Stories I Tell My Family and Friends

Stories I Tell
My Family and Friends

The Memoirs of
U.S. Senator James T. Broyhill

ISBN: 978-1-7347964-9-0

compiled by Randell Jones
Daniel Boone Footsteps Publishing
Winston-Salem, NC
www.DanielBooneFootsteps.com

The best epitaph is
a life well lived ...

... in respect of those who molded it
and lovingly remembered
by those it touched.

Preface

My father entertained friends and family for years with stories of his fascinating and long life, and he began recording some of these stories in writing at least forty years ago. I had been urging him for years to compile these memories into a book but it was not until the fall of 2022, five months before he died, that he began to focus in earnest on the project. Sadly, he passed away at age 95 on February 18, 2023, before the project was completed. One of his last requests to me was to publish his memoirs, but to note within them that he had more to say. In addition to his own writings dating from years ago to more recent transcriptions, sections contributed after his death by friends and colleagues are included.

James Thomas Broyhill

Dad treasured his friendships, and his friends knew that he loved to tell stories, not only about his life but also about historical figures. He could enthrall any group with jokes from his extensive repertoire which had been used to embellish many political speeches over the years. He could completely captivate a large crowd or a small gathering of friends with a humorous story, holding the attention of his audience until the punchline, always getting a huge response, and joining in the laughter with gusto! He enjoyed reading and reciting history, and made the past come alive. Even at age 95, he could recite all of the U.S. Presidents and Vice Presidents, and could tell you the King or Queen of England at any point in time. Rotary Clubs and other organizations often asked him to give his PowerPoint lectures on the history of the U.S. Capitol, the Battle of Kings Mountain, and U.S. presidents. He enjoyed taking visitors to Washington on a tour of the U.S. Capitol, and his knowledge of the artwork, historical figures who had graced the halls of Congress since the beginning of our nation, and architectural details of that building were exceeded only by his gratitude and appreciation for those whose ideals and sacrifices built our democracy. Dad had a front row seat in the making of much legislative history and was honored to serve his country for more than a quarter of a century, both in Washington, D.C., and in North Carolina.

I would like to thank those who spoke and officiated at Dad's funeral: Reverends Glenn Kinken, Craig Ford, Michael Brown, and David Smith; Governor Jim Martin, Senator Richard Burr, Jack Roemer, Dr. Bill McCall, Senator Phil Kirk, Randell Jones (editor and publisher of these memoirs), my brother Ed Broyhill, representatives of the Overmountain Victory Trail Association, and all of Dad's six grandchildren. Our family was honored that Governor Cooper lowered American flags in the state of North Carolina on the day of Dad's funeral, and that hundreds paid their final respects for him, in person and through heartfelt letters.

Thanks to all who contributed to this book by writing sections, editing, and offering assistance. Susan Shinn Turner spent hours transcribing Dad's oral memories. Phil Kirk gave valuable insights and advice. Susan Cobb contacted the Senate and House of Representatives to obtain official lists of Dad's former staff. He wanted the list to be complete, and I apologize for any name that was unintentionally omitted. I deeply appreciate the support from my husband, Bob Beach, my nephew, Penn Broyhill, and his wife Natalie who assisted in editing text and choosing and organizing photographs for this book and Dad's funeral reception, and my cousin Anne Stevens Hsu for her collaboration and sharing of our family history and photographs she contributed from over thirty years of meticulous research, publication, and documentation.

— Marilyn Broyhill Beach

Foreword
by Phil Kirk

For six decades, I have admired Senator Jim Broyhill as a family man, furniture executive, civic and community leader, member of the United States House of Representatives and Senate, North Carolina's Secretary of Commerce, and now as North Carolina's premier elder statesman.

I was pleased to learn that Senator Broyhill had decided to write his memoirs so that family, friends, and historians could read of his many experiences on the local, state, and national levels.

Phil Kirk and daughters with Rep. James T. Broyhill, c1980

In "Stories I Tell My Family and Friends," Senator Broyhill shares with you about his early life, his entry into Republican politics, and his 25 years of service in Washington, D.C. You will learn what factors have shaped his amazing life, what his key beliefs are, in addition to the advice he gives to newcomers to public office. He also relates some important legislative wins in his stellar career and offers insights on the presidents he has known. He comments on his political opponents, as well as his work in Raleigh as Secretary of Commerce and as the co-chairman of the Work First Business Council at its inception. He also shares some humorous (and true) stories about life in the spotlight.

I know you are eager to begin reading this book. First, however, I want to share some of my experiences with Senator Broyhill; his wife, Louise; daughter, Marilyn Broyhill Beach and husband Bob; son, Ed and wife Melanie; and the couple's grandchildren and great-grandchildren.

My first involvement with Senator Broyhill came in his first campaign for Congress in 1962. I was president of the East Rowan Teenage Republicans and supported my county chairman in the GOP primary. I had never met the man from Lenoir who was soon to become the Congressman! He defeated his opponent in the primary with about 80 percent of the vote. The day after the primary, I called the winner and promised him that the Teen Age Republicans in Rowan County would work hard for him and we did, delivering more than 5,000 Broyhill brochures, sugar scoops, and cookbooks door-to-door.

On Election Day, we were all excited about Congressman Broyhill's upset victory over a long-time incumbent Democrat congressman. Many called that campaign a family affair because of the involvement of wife Louise, whom some said was the best campaigner in the family! I volunteered in future Broyhill campaigns and then became chairman of the Rowan County GOP before being elected to the North Carolina Senate in 1970, thanks in part to Broyhill's mentorship.

We continued working together with new Republican governor, Jim Holshouser, a close friend of the Broyhills. The couple was carrying the banner for North Carolina on Capitol Hill while I was serving as the chief of staff for the first Republican governor of North Carolina in nearly a century. After Holshouser's term ended in 1976, Congressman Broyhill invited me to move to Washington to become his chief of staff, where I served for seven years. During this period, I worked closely with the Congressman. My admiration for him grew and grew, and I learned a lot.

Senator Broyhill preached and taught the value of hard work. He ended many of his speeches this way: "There are three ingredients for a successful political campaign. Number one is hard work. Number two is hard work. Number three is hard work."

He applied the same philosophy to his congressional service, and he expected his staff to do the same. While he was recognized as an effective legislator who could actually get things done even though he never served in the majority, he realized that the key to being re-elected was quality constituent service. He knew that getting Social Security benefits, solving problems for active servicemen and servicewomen and for veterans, securing passports, and other government services — in addition to going to county fairs, riding in parades, and holding office hours in every town in the district — were what the voters saw and what they appreciated.

Several of our current Republican congressmen and senators told me that Congressman Broyhill taught them the importance of constituent service. He also did this for many members of Congress from throughout the country when they first arrived in D.C., including former House Speaker Newt Gingrich.

Senator Broyhill was not reallly big on introducing bills every day or every week. He did not feel he earned his pay by the number of bills he sponsored. However, as the top Republican on the powerful Energy and Commerce committee, he was known for his effectiveness in working with Congressman John Dingell, who chaired the committee.

During my early tenure in the Washington office, the Congressman told me on several Mondays and Fridays that he was leaving the office to go on an environmental field trip. That made perfect sense to me because the environment was an important part of his committee work. It did not take too long for me to realize that the "environmental field trip" was a round of golf!

While Senator Broyhill is a proud and influential Republican, he never let partisan politics enter his congressional office. He and his staff worked as hard to solve problems for Democrats as they did for the Republican faithful. In fact, sometimes he was teased good-naturedly for working harder to help a partisan Democrat who would never vote for him than he did for his friends. That was not true, but he treated everyone alike, no matter what their political views were or their social status, gender, or color.

That could explain why he won election in so many counties that had never voted for a Republican. He was gerrymandered several times in an effort to defeat him. One time the state ended up with two additional Republican congressmen. Another time he was pitted against an entrenched Democrat incumbent whose district included very few locally elected Republicans. Now most, if not all, of those counties elect far more Republicans than Democrats. Jim Broyhill made it respectable to be a Republican.

Over the years and in a variety of capacities, I have asked people for adjectives they would use to describe the Lenoir native. Here is some of what I heard:

sincere, honest, gracious, hardworking, loyal, smart, dedicated, compassionate, caring. He is often called sharp as a tack! I recently asked him what I should say to people who ask about him and his response was, "Tell them I can still name the *vice* presidents in order and backwards!"

I hope I have given you an idea of why I admire Senator Broyhill so much. I knew in working for him that he would never embarrass me or any member of his family or staff. That cannot be said about many elected officials these days. I could write much more about Senator Broyhill; however, thanks to the Senator himself, you can read this book and learn much, much more about this giant of a man.

I call him the real G-E-M (pronounced Jim) ... a rare find in today's world — a real jewel!

Career-long friends, Jim Broyhill and Phil Kirk

Table of Contents

Introduction

by Jim Broyhill

It was noontime, January 3, 1963. I was in the big city of Washington, D.C., and this was a day my life was going to change forever. I was in the United States Capitol building, in the House of Representatives, and about to be sworn in as a United States Congressman.

Just that past November, I had been elected to Congress from North Carolina's 9th congressional district after a long, hard-fought campaign, winning out over a ten-year veteran congressman, Hugh Alexander of Kannapolis. At that moment, I had no idea that the United States Capitol was to be my address for the next 24 years.

United States Congress,
January 3, 1963

I served in the Congress from 1963 until 1986, when North Carolina Governor Jim Martin appointed me to the seat left vacant by the death of Senator John East. I was unsuccessful in my bid for reelection and retired from Congress in 1986. Soon after, Governor Martin asked me to come to Raleigh and take the position of state Secretary of Commerce and Chairman of the North Carolina Economic Development Commission.

From that day in 1963 when I left Broyhill Furniture Company to pursue a different direction from my brother Paul, I knew I made the right decision. We were brothers and from the same background, but we each had different talents and interests. Though our career paths diverged, we both followed in our father's footsteps. My dad had been passionate about Republican politics and was active on local, state, and national fronts. He was proud of my work in the House and later in the Senate. Paul carried on Dad's business and took it to a level of incredible success. Because our parents placed within us a sense of commitment, we both intensely approached our different fields with a feeling of obligation to our constituents: my voters, his employees.

I have been extremely fortunate over the years to have had people working on my staff and volunteering on my campaigns who have contributed to my success, enriched my life, and made me look good! I am profoundly grateful to all.

One thing has not changed and that is the value of good friends. Friendship isn't always easy to describe. The dictionary defines "friend" as a close acquaintance, a person whom one knows well and is fond of. So, as I think of the word "friend," I think of simple adjectives. We have close friend, dear friend, childhood friend, trusted friend, golfing friend, and so forth. No matter which adjective you use, everyone understands the meaning of the word "friend." Friends are special people. We can't pick our family. We are limited in that respect. But we can pick our friends. And our friends can be just as diverse as the adjectives we use to describe our friends. Our friends, in a very real sense, reflect the choices we have made in life.

I have lived far beyond my biblically allotted three score and ten. However, I would never trade my friends, my wonderful life, and my great family for less gray hair or a flatter belly.

Early Life and Family

by Jim Broyhill

Born in 1927, I grew up in the small town of Lenoir, N.C., during the 1930s and early 1940s. I will always have fond and nostalgic memories of those years. I was the third child of James Edgar and Satie Hunt Broyhill. My sister Allene and brother, Paul, were older than I. Bettie, my younger sister, was 18 months younger. The fact that I had to repeat the fourth grade because of an illness meant that Bettie and I were only one class apart all through school, and thus we were much closer to each other than to the other siblings. In fact, we often double dated during our high school years. My older sister, Allene, finished high school six years before I did. She had graduated from Converse College and was married well before I graduated from high school. My school years with Paul overlapped only one year, 1940-41.

James Edgar and Satie Hunt Broyhill

My Mother and Father

My mother, Satie Hunt Broyhill, was a take-charge woman, especially in taking care of others. This was said at her funeral: If you went to the front porch and found a bag of apples or a vase of roses, you knew Satie Broyhill had been there. She loved music and was an accomplished pianist, having studied music at what is now Appalachian State University. She delivered roses from her gardens to friends who needed cheering up. Her swimming pool was open to a large group of family and friends. Mother excelled at entertaining friends and furniture customers, and family gatherings for her sixteen grandchildren.

Early Life and Family

3

Satie Broyhill was born in Genesee, Pennsylvania, right on the border of New York State. Her grandmother was of Dutch descent and her name derived from the Dutch spelling of "Sadie." Her great-grandfather Harris fought for the Union during the Civil War, having been given $300 to replace a wealthy man who did not want to be drafted. The family bought a farm with the money.

Hartley Hunt Family

Mother's father, Hartley Hunt, was also born in New York State and later moved to Genesee, Pennsylvania. He was employed by W. J. Grandin. In 1911, Grandin came to Caldwell County and bought 75,000 acres, which ranged from the Yadkin River in Caldwell County north to Watauga County north to what is now the Blue Ridge Parkway. He formed a community named Grandin between Wilkes County and Lenoir and set up a sawmill and planing mill. He built a railroad from Wilkesboro to Grandin as well as a hotel, a store, houses for the workers, and a church. It was a thriving community. Grandfather Hunt was sent from Pennsylvania to Grandin to be the forestry manager. It was his job to look after the timber and the forest, to make sure no one was poaching, and to get the lumber to the mill. He brought his three daughters, including my mother who was 13 at the time, with him to this new community.

Satie Hunt with siblings

Hartley wanted his daughters to have the best possible education. He had heard about Watauga Academy / Appalachian Training School (later to become Appalachian State University) which had been started in 1899, coincidentally on the date of my mother's birth, July 13. He decided to send Satie there to continue her education.

My father was born in 1892 and was raised in the Wilkes
County township of Boomer, about fifteen miles from
Grandin. His father, Isaac Broyhill, was a farmer, and his older
brother Tom had a business cutting timber and selling the
lumber to fledgling furniture companies in North Wilkesboro
and Lenoir. Dad would work for his brother, occasionally, but
would mostly work for his father on the farm.

James Edgar
leaves the farm

Dad was ambitious. He rented some bottom land and planted
corn to expand the income on the farm. The spring floods
came along and washed his crop out. That's when he decided
there had to be a better way to make a living than farming. He
found his way to Boone and to the Watauga Appalachian
Training School for Teachers in 1913 with very little money in
his pocket — a $5 gold piece. He was 21 years of age, trying to further his
education, having only completed six grades of school. Dr. Blandford B.
Dougherty, the school's president, took a chance on him, and put him in the
seventh grade. He also arranged for Dad to get janitorial, barbering, and other
odd jobs so that he could support himself financially.

My parents met at the school. They were in the same grade, despite their age
difference. One of the ways Dad got Mother's attention was by asking, "Would
you like your pencil sharpened?" (All of the farm boys carried jackknives.) My
father's education was interrupted when he
was drafted for service in WWI. He had not
quite finished army training when he came
down with a case of mumps. He was sent to
Walter Reed Hospital. When he recovered, he
was put back into another unit to train to go
overseas, only to be sent again to Walter Reed
with a diagnosis of tuberculosis. While there
he took two courses. One was photography,
and for the rest of his life, whenever you saw
him, he had a camera in his hand. He loved to
take pictures. The other course he took was
typing. That became important after he was
discharged in 1919 and sought work with his
brother Tom who had started a furniture
company. Tom put my father to work in the
office because of the skills he had learned in

James Edgar Broyhill

school and the army, such as double-entry bookkeeping and typing.

By this time, Mr. Grandin's empire had ended up in receivership. In 1916, rain and floods had washed out the railroad. Furthermore, when the war ended wood products were not as much in demand. My grandfather Hunt was appointed as the local manager to help sell the property to repay the creditors.

Dad made his way to Grandin to see my mother after the war was over and they married in 1921, settling in Lenoir. Together they raised a family of four children and helped build the furniture company that later became Broyhill Furniture Industries, once the largest privately held furniture company in the world.

James Edgar and Satie Hunt Broyhill wedding photo

My Siblings

Allene

My sister was my oldest sibling, born in 1922. She was always highly successful in school, very popular, and beautiful. She married Bill Stevens in 1944. They had a happy marriage with six children. Those children were a blessing to her for her entire life. Allene was a philanthropist in the community. She gave generously to many worthwhile charities in Lenoir, particularly in the arts.

She had a wonderful outlook on life. I include her philosophy of life here.

My philosophy of life
by Allene Broyhill Stevens, sister of Jim Broyhill

• The three L's for living: Love God. Love your fellow man. Live usefully.
• Think positively. Attitude is a choice. You can be negative or positive about almost anything.
• Laugh often, especially at yourself.

Jim, Allene, Paul, and Bettie

- Never stop learning. Be curious — open your mind to new ideas, new experiences.
- Eat healthily. Exercise regularly. Get a good night's sleep.
- Listen more than you speak. You don't have to say everything you think.
- Smile often. Say "thank you" often and mean it.
- Do not waste two of your most valuable resources — your time and your money.
- Do not be a worrier. Most of the time, things will figure themselves out.
- Allow love to rule your life, to guide your thoughts, to dictate your words, and to inspire your deeds.

Paul

My brother Paul was the head of Broyhill Furniture. His management style led to success of the company. First, he had a great sense of style, and was able to keep the furniture line fresh looking and sellable from the standards of retail. Second, his management technique was unique. Every year, he would have the managers, the people who headed up a profit center in the company, stand up in front of their peers, and report what they had done in the past year to further production, profit, and safety, and to reduce loss. They then told the group their goals for the coming year, and Paul would ensure that those goals were accomplished.

(I'm told that this was the same management tool Jack Welch used with General Electric.) Paul and his wife Faye had three children.

Paul decided to forgo his senior year at [Lenoir High School] and to attend Culver Military Academy. He was probably one of the few senior plebes in the history of Culver. However, I am sure that the experience was greatly responsible for Paul's achieving membership in Phi Beta Kappa when he went to Carolina a few years later. He told me that the only way he could avoid the hazing and harassment of a plebe was to stay in his room and study. I believe those study habits stayed with him throughout his college career and beyond. …

Around 1946, Paul was discharged from the Army. He immediately re-enrolled at Chapel Hill, where he had already finished one year of college. Paul and I were at Carolina together for two years. Although we did not take classes together, we saw each other every day at the Phi Delta Theta house, where we were members. We both took our meals there. As I recall, Paul and I took two big trips together while we were at Chapel Hill. One trip was to New York on the train, and another was by car to the Republican National Convention that was held in Philadelphia. While in Philadelphia, we met many Republican Party leaders of the time including Senator Bob Taft, Governor Thomas Dewey, Congressman Carroll Reese of Tennessee, the chairman of the Republican National Committee, and many others.

I remember an incident that occurred on the way to Philadelphia. Throughout his lifetime, Paul enjoyed telling stories about how tight I was with money. On that occasion we were passing through Colonial Heights, just north of Petersburg, Virginia, on U.S. Highway 1. I was driving when a siren sounded behind us, and I was stopped for speeding. Paul was asleep in the passenger seat. I remember nudging him and saying, "Wake up and pay the man!" I didn't have a cent on me.

Bettie

My younger sister, Bettie and I were close in age and were together often, particularly in high school. We were both members of the band and shared friends. We usually rode our bicycles to school together. After our marriages, our families lived next door to each other for a number of years. She had four children.

Bettie and Jim

Early Life

Cora

Cora (Carrie) Horton was born and raised in the mountains of Wilkes County. She came to Lenoir around 1918. She was extremely important to me and to our entire family. Not only

Jim taking his first measure of the world

did she help to raise me, because Mother and Dad traveled a lot, but she instilled values, love, and discipline in my early life. Cora lived in the Broyhill house for over 50 years and was one of the most gifted cooks I have ever known. She was especially known for her chocolate chip cookies and her apple pie. I remember listening to the Joe Lewis-Max Snelling fight on her radio with her and my little sister Bettie.

Etta Powell, also greatly loved and appreciated, helped take care of my children — Marilyn, Ed, and Philip — both in Lenoir and Washington.

Etta Powell with Cora Horton
at a family wedding

Rheumatic Fever

In 1937, I came home from school one day with a sore throat. It turned out to be strep throat. That turned into rheumatic fever, which affects the heart. My doctors expected me to die, and my family got on their knees to pray.

Dr. Caroline McNairy had delivered me. She was also my physician. At that time, a doctor who had received his training at Johns Hopkins came back to Lenoir

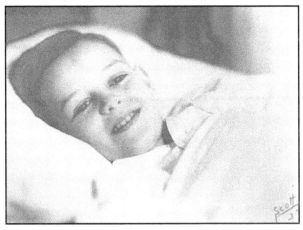

Jim suffered with rheumatic fever

Early Life and Family

to practice. He had learned about sulfa drugs. You could take it internally, and during WWII it was developed as a powder to be used by medics to aid against gangrene. Dr. McNairy consulted with the doctor from Johns Hopkins about the sulfa drug, and I took it internally. My fever broke and finally went down. My family's prayers were answered.

My feet did not touch the ground for five months. My parents would not let me out of bed because the doctors were concerned about my heart. Later, I had to learn to walk again. I can't remember the early parts of my illness because I was in a coma.

As the summer came along, my parents wanted me to get out in the sunshine, for Vitamin D! They put me out in a bed in the front yard. All my little 10-year-old friends would see me out in the yard and come by and visit. We had a lot of boys in the neighborhood. In those days, we had woods beside our house, a great place for kids to play. Before my illness and after my year of recuperation, we built treehouses there. Those were wonderful days.

I repeated the fourth grade, and from then on, I was a year older than the other kids in my class. I'm convinced today that's one of the things that gave me the maturity for leadership

Jim with his parents

roles in high school and later in the community. So, history shows that my bout with rheumatic fever was not all that detrimental to me. I was able to make a positive out of it.

After finishing the six grades at East Harper Elementary School, I went to the seventh grade, located at that time in the same building as Lenoir High School. Thus, we junior high kids had daily contact with the older kids. I began playing the flute and piccolo and was in training to become a member of the famous Lenoir High School Band. I chose the flute because that was the instrument Paul played.

At the end of the seventh grade, the students who qualified were admitted to the senior band. To qualify, a student had to be able to play his instrument competently and to march expertly, because the LHS band was also a superior marching band. In the early spring of 1941, I was admitted to the senior band and was a proud member of the flute section.

Lenoir High School Band

L et me digress here to explain a little more about the famous Lenoir High School Band. The band was started in the mid-1920s. After WWI, the local American Legion, an organization formed after WWI the war to represent veterans, had sponsored a community band. When interest in the effort waned, the Legion donated the instruments to the high school for the purpose of organizing a school band. Captain James C. Harper, a local businessman and an Army veteran of World War I, had been active in the American Legion band. He volunteered his time to conduct the high school band. It was not long before Captain Harper became the permanent director. He spent the rest of his life dedicated to teaching young people to play instruments and to teaching us some of life's lessons. He drew the analogy between the personal discipline we needed to master our instruments and the necessity to play in tandem with other instruments, to the skills we needed to be successful in life. He ran the band with military precision.

Capt. Harper was married to Charlotte Critz, whose father was secretary/treasurer to R.J. Reynolds Tobacco Co. Her mother Lucy was sister to R.J. Reynolds. Capt. Harper's family founded Lenoir and they had the first businesses there, including Harper Furniture, the first furniture company in town.

"There's James Broyhill. He Plays the Flute."

James Christian Phofl was the son of a Moravian bishop and grew up in Winston-Salem. He was well known in music circles. For example, he started the James Christian Phofl Music Program at Brevard College in Brevard, N.C., in the 1950s.

This story takes place in Charlotte in 1945, when Dr. Phofl was the director of Davidson-Queens Symphony Orchestra. He knew me because I had played for him at music camp at Queens College, and at Easter programs in Winston-Salem. I played for the sunrise and evening services.

One afternoon during rehearsals, I was there waiting for a friend of mine who was playing in the orchestra. Dr. Phofl said to me, "Have you got your flute with you? I need you for the concert tonight. The first-chair flutist didn't show up."

I was 15. I did have my flute with me and said, "I can do that, but I need to look at the music."

"Can you get a tuxedo?" he asked.

I had enough time to go rent a tuxedo, and I sight-read the concert that night. That's how much confidence Dr. Pholf had in me, and I'm proud about that. A newspaper headline from the event reads, "Orchestra finds flutist in audience; show goes on." As a senior in high school, I also played as first-chair flutist with the North Carolina Symphony.

the important story of patriot militiamen pursuing a British force that became the Battle of Kings Mountain, a turning point in the War for American Independence. My father considered his role in establishing the Overmountain Victory Trail as part of the U.S. National Trails System to be among his most important contributions during his 24 years of Congressional service. Randell has contributed his book to your library in memory of Senator Broyhill. You will also find a free video about the founding of the OVNHT and Congressman Broyhill's role in that effort, "Remembering How We Got Here," at BecomingAmerica250.com. Find it under "1780" under "History Highlights." And with it, find free access to the "New Kings Mountain Story Video Trilogy," which may also interest your patrons.

Sincerely,

Marilyn

Marilyn Broyhill Beach

Marilyn Broyhill Beach

2841 Reynolds Drive

Winston-Salem, North Carolina 27104

336-414-9855

marilynbroyhillbeach@gmail.com

July 5, 2024

Dear Librarian:

Enclosed are two complimentary books for your library. One is the memoirs of my father, Jim Broyhill, former U.S. Congressman and Senator, who passed away in 2023 at age 95. He entitled his memoirs, "Stories I Tell My Family and Friends." He did not finish the project before his death, but I have edited his writing with the help of Randell Jones, historian, author, editor, and Dad's friend, who has compiled the stories Dad did complete with additional pieces written by friends and colleagues into this collection. I am pleased to share this with your library's patrons.

The accompanying book is "A Guide to the Overmountain Victory National Historic Trail," written by Randell Jones with a foreword by Jim Broyhill. It tells

Where is that flute today?
After 1946, I donated my flute to the Lenoir High School band.
It was a silver-plated, open-hole French flute. You covered the holes
with your fingers. I was able to get a deep sound with that flute.
I couldn't play now, because you need to develop a strong
embouchure — the technique of using your lips, facial muscles,
tongue, and teeth in playing a wind instrument.

The flute first went to Katherine Menefee Price, a graduate of the
Juilliard School in New York City. Her students have graduated from
conservatories and universities throughout the country. Katherine
eventually passed the flute to her sister, Mattie Menafee, of Winston-
Salem. She married Milton Rhodes, also of Winston Salem. He was
the head of the arts center for many years. Today, the Milton Rhodes
Center for the Arts is named for him.

I was in the Glee Club at Lenoir High
School, and later was in the choir at
First Baptist Church in Lenoir.
I sang second tenor, which had the
lead in the men's quartet. We also
had a men's octet. As a freshman at
the University of North Carolina,
Chapel Hill, I joined the men's cho-
rus. Andy Griffith was a senior and
was club President. My vocal range
was about one octave. I could get up
to F and as low as E on a good day.

Jim in high school

People of Significance

Who are the people that you remember?
You remember the people who had an influence in your life.
You don't remember the celebrities of yesterday.

Who won the Oscar four years ago?
Now talk about your first-grade teacher. We all remember!

First grade: Evelyn McGuire Allen (Mrs. Austin Allen)
Second grade: Miss Esther Howard
Third grade: Miss Hickerson
Fourth grade: Mrs. Dudley Rabb, Miss Agnes Cloninger
Fifth grade: Miss Myers
Sixth grade Mrs. Julia Kinlaw (Mrs. Rudy Kinlaw)
Seventh grade: Miss Mary Angley
Eighth grade: Mrs. Lucille Rector, Miss Eunice Query, librarian
High school: Ralph and Pauline Laney, Virginia Cobb, and
Capt. James Harper, George Kirsten, and Bob Klepfer, band.
Eleventh grade: Mrs. C.J. Goodman; Elizabeth McConnell Jarrett,
English; Miss Haley
Twelfth grade: Miss Lillian E. Sisk

Learning To Work

by Jim Broyhill

During high school, I took my first job at the old Collins-Pridmore department store on West Avenue in uptown Lenoir during the Christmas season of 1942. In the spring of 1943, I took a weekend job at Smithey's department store. Founded in the late 1800s by E.J. Smithey of Wilkesboro, Smithey's was a small chain with locations in Wilkesboro, Lenoir, Taylorsville, Sparta, and West Jefferson. Smithey catered to the country trade. Those were the folks who came into town on weekends from the country to conduct their business.

The store was adjacent to "Hog Waller," which was an area where the country people parked their vehicles and sold or traded wares, animals, or garden produce.

Smithey's sold merchandise at discounted prices. The idea of self-help or self-serve shopping was a new concept found at larger grocery chains such as Winn-Dixie and Piggly Wiggly. On the contrary, Smithey's still used the old system: customers came in the door, gave you a list of what they wanted, and you got up the order, added up the cost, collected for the order, and put the cash in the cash register. When I worked there, it was the era of rationing, so we had the added responsibility of collecting ration stamps for certain items such as sugar.

Lenoir has preserved parts of its historic downtown cityscape

Not long after I began working at Smithey's, Jim Odell, manager of Winn-Dixie, offered me a job with a substantial raise in pay. He offered to pay me 25 cents an hour, so I jumped at it. There, the shopper used a grocery cart and gathered his own items from the shelves, then took them to a checkout counter to make payment.

courtesy Bill Tate

At mid 20th Century, Lenoir was already a busy community with good jobs

I did some bagging of groceries, but soon Jim had me stocking the shelves and operating a section of the store where customers could check their purchases, go on about town to do other shopping, and come back later to pick them up. I was in charge of keeping track of the checked bags.

In early 1944, my father asked me to come to his office to help out with a chore or two. Before long, I resigned my job at Winn-Dixie and went to Dad's office just about every day after school and on Saturdays. Back in those days, the office was open and fully staffed every Saturday from 8 a.m. until noon.

Like keeping up with the checked bags at Winn-Dixie, the first job I had at Broyhill was to keep track of the sales quota system. At the outset of World War II, Dad found that due to shortages and increased demand, he could sell anything he made. He easily could have sold his entire output to just a few retailers in the larger markets. However, Dad decided early on that his output was going to be divided among all his customers who had bought from him and who had been loyal to him in the past. So, he developed an intricate system to keep track of the sales to each customer. That was long before the days of computers. We established a dollar quota for everyone, and I manually entered the dollar amount of every order for every customer onto a card system.

Not long thereafter, I was given a far more responsible job in the purchasing office. I prepared every invoice for payment. I verified the purchase, checked it for accuracy, obtained receiving reports from the factory to assure it had arrived, and attached the report to any freight bills. Then, I entered the information by hand in a ledger with the vendor's name, product, amount, and accounting for the purchase: cost of goods or capital goods. Before I got the hang of it, I charged off some sewing machines as cost of goods rather than putting them in the capital column.

In early 1944, Dad had the idea that I should get some actual experience selling furniture on the road. Like my brother, Paul, I had attended most summer markets at Chicago and at High Point with Dad since 1938, so I was familiar with the line and, of course, knew every Broyhill salesman and many of the major customers.

Dad gave me two territories to cover: eastern North Carolina and eastern Virginia. Talmadge Biddix, Dad's former driver, had been promoted into sales and had become a seasoned salesman in Lenoir. He and I scrounged some rationed gasoline stamps and started out. In Virginia, we covered Richmond, Norfolk, Newport News, Charlottesville, Lynchburg, and the towns in the Shenandoah Valley. From there, we moved down into North Carolina, covering Raleigh and everything east. What a great experience that was, and we didn't have to work to sell a thing! Everyone welcomed us with open arms and took any product we gave them, even if it were only two or three suites of furniture and a half-dozen chairs. However, we made a lot of friends for the Company. We were just about the only salespeople they had seen in months.

I must hasten to add that this was all before the days of the consolidated Broyhill Furniture Industries. We had more than one order blank. Every company was a separate corporation, except for the two Lenoir Chair companies, one bedroom plant, and one upholstering plant. So, each company's order had to go on a separate order blank: Harper Furniture on Harper, Otis Broyhill Furniture of Marion on another, and so on.

After that first trip with Talmadge Biddix, I started taking trips through the two territories on my own. I worked the summer markets and waited on customers who attended from those two territories. In those days we didn't show many goods. We didn't have to. We could sell everything we made by telephone. However, Dad encouraged the salesmen to make goodwill contact with the customers, saying, "Boys, the war will be over soon, and I want them to remember who you are and who took care of them when things were in short supply."

In 1946, we started showing the line again at the High Point market (not Chicago), although we did not have much trouble selling the output from the factories. Since the war was over, demand for furniture increased as veterans were back starting families and setting up housekeeping in their new homes. That was when I was saddled with the responsibility of getting the samples ready for the shows and making sure the showrooms were set up for market.

All through college, on weekends and during the summer months, I continued to serve territory sixteen: eastern North Carolina. We employed a young man, Kemp Honeycutt from Hickory, North Carolina, to take over the eastern Virginia territory, and he did a fine job. However, in the late '40s, we decided that the territory needed a permanent man, and we hired Tommy Culbreath, a young man Paul and I had gotten to know at Carolina. Tommy had worked his way through school doing various jobs. He had a personality that fit in well with the customers in the eastern part of the state. I was still helping out, making sure the market samples were prepared and the market showrooms set up. Paul also did some traveling in those territories. Both of us called on dealers all across the country. My brother-in-law Bill Stevens played a valuable role in the business as well and worked with Paul and me as a team.

As the tastes of the average furniture consumer changed, we had to work harder to make a sale. The company had to pay more attention to styling and design. Paul had a flair for that part of the business and early on began spending more and more time working with the design team to streamline the line and to merchandise it. Our line was neither the lowest-priced line in the business nor the highest-priced line. We had a nice niche in the middle and that is where we stayed through the years, offering a line of well-styled furniture that fit the taste and the budget of middle-income Americans.

The College Years

The only thing I regret about my college experience is that I was a mediocre student. I made all As and Bs in high school, and I made the honor roll. But in college, I did not make the extra effort because I loved to play golf. I made Bs and Cs. In fact, I seldom bought a book. I attended classes and took notes. I was not a party boy, and I did not drink. In fact, I was a senior in college in 1949 before I had my first glass of wine.

I joined Phi Delta Theta fraternity. I had some other offers, but this was the one I chose. My brother was a member, and a lot of the members were the Durham boys that I knew. I don't remember any hazing, which I never liked.

Our fraternity had a sizable number of returning veterans, and many had seen combat. As I recall, we had close to 100 veterans— a big group. From time to time, those who enjoyed beer liked to have a beer party. But I was dry. There were several of us who didn't drink and who didn't like to be assessed for providing the beer at the parties. We would voice our concerns, but we always got outvoted!

I told a fraternity brother that I loved to play golf, and he said, "Why don't you join Hope Valley Country Club? You can get a student membership." I made my application and was glad to find out the dues were only $100 a year, plus the food bill every month. I didn't eat there much, however. In those days, we carried our own bags. Looking back, if not for my love of golf I would not have met my pretty wife, Louise.

Summer of 1947 — Transatlantic Voyage to Europe on the Queen Elizabeth I

We were Baptists and were part of the Baptist World Alliance, a worldwide alliance of Baptist churches who got together once a year. A gathering was to be held in Copenhagen in the summer of 1947. My father wanted to go. Some members of our church also wanted to go but could not afford the trip. This is not well known, but Dad quietly offered to pay their way. One of the church members was a supervisor in our office who had lost her brother in a tank battle in WWII. She wanted to visit her brother's gravesite in France. Another was a young preacher who was just starting work in the church; he wanted to go, and my father also paid his way.

This was the maiden voyage of the Queen Elizabeth I ocean liner after the war. She had ferried troops back and forth between Europe and America. After the war, the ship was put in dry dock and refurbished to be an ocean liner. As we got aboard ship, my father got an urgent message that his brother Thomas had suffered a heart attack, so he went back to Lenoir to be with him. My mother, sister Bettie, and I proceeded with the journey.

When we arrived in London, the evidence of the war was prominent. It had been bombed out. Rubble was everywhere, and food was scarce. Then we boarded a train and went through Hamburg. The city had been completely flattened. We didn't get out, but we saw it. It had been bombed to smithereens — nothing there. We continued to Copenhagen where there was daily preaching. I didn't go to all of it! I became a tourist.

One of the men we met in Copenhagen was a prominent Baptist preacher from Richmond who was elected president of the Alliance that year. He had his family with him, and we kept up with them over the years. One son became an attorney in Richmond; he became a lobbyist in the 1960s and was in my office quite a lot.

We extended the trip to visit Switzerland and Paris. Switzerland had not been touched that much by war, so that was where we had the best food. Paris was bleak. It was very dark at night and didn't have many lights around. That's one of the things I remember. We went to the museums, the Louvre and so forth. I remember seeing the Mona Lisa.

That's the Girl for Me

by Jim Broyhill

Louise Robbins went to Hollins College from 1947 to 1949, and then transferred to Carolina (UNC-Chapel Hill). At that time, I was a senior, and she was a junior. I had met her twice before, at the Phi Delta Theta House, but the third encounter was the most significant. That one "took."

Louise Robbins

I was in my 1949 Plymouth going down Franklin Street and saw two gorgeous girls standing in front of Spencer Dorm at a bus stop. I came to a screeching halt. The girls were Lou Carmichael (later Eshelman) and Louise Robbins. I knew Lou better because she had dated my roommate. They were going to Durham, where both girls lived. I said, "Hop in, I'll take you."

I got the directions and headed down Franklin Street to Durham.
Louise leaned over and said, "Where are you going?"
"I'm going to play golf," I said.
"I love to golf," she said.
I thought, *That's the girl for me.*

I saw her the next day and asked her for a date. She said she was busy that night. She was dating every boy in Chapel Hill. It was something. I figured, well, maybe she didn't want to date me. Then she came running down the sidewalk and said, "Please call me again." So I did. I booked her up so the other boys couldn't get in. It turned out that she didn't really love golf, but that didn't matter. She was the girl for me.

I graduated and went back to the furniture business. Even during college, I had been a traveling salesman for the company. My father started me early. I had a territory in eastern North Carolina — from Durham to eastern cities such as Wilmington, Elizabeth City, and Greenville. I had trained a young man for a month or more, but he was drafted, so we had to have somebody cover that territory. I took over in 1950 but tried to visit Durham on the weekends. Louise's mother said, "Why don't you stay with us when you are in town?" Every Friday, Louise had to date me because I was a guest in her house in the beautiful Forest Hills neighborhood. Her mother was my ally.

Louise, My Bride

Louise had another year of college, and we got married June 2, 1951, the day she graduated. She did not participate in her graduation ceremony because we had a busy week of wedding parties. We married at Louise's home church in Durham, Trinity Methodist, and our reception was at Hope Valley Country Club. I played at Hope Valley Country Club for 3-1/2 years, and for a year-and-a-half after my graduation until they caught up with me and said, "You're no longer a student." About that time, I got married, and then I went to Hope Valley on Louise's father's membership.

Wedding Day Eve
Jim, Louise, and J.E. Broyhill, Jim's father

June 2, 1951

70th Wedding Anniversary

That's the Girl for Me

Our Children

Jim and Louise with Philip, Marilyn, and Ed (1967)

Marilyn

Marilyn was born in 1952. She is smart, loving, and so helpful. Marilyn went to three great schools. For high school, she went to the National Cathedral School for Girls, the most prestigious school in Washington, Stanford University for her undergraduate degree and then graduated from Columbia University Law School. Her husband Bob Beach had graduated from Dartmouth and was an officer in the Navy during the Vietnam War. He came back after discharge to Stanford, where he earned a double degree in law and a master's in business. Bob and Marilyn met at Stanford and married in 1974.

They had a beautiful wedding in Lenoir. Bob was from Madison, Wisconsin. His parents and many of their friends came. One of their close friends who came was Oscar Mayer. The night before we had a beautiful party at Cedar Rock Country Club. I had engaged an award-winning clogging group from Newland in Avery County. They put on a show for us and got everybody up to do clogging. I'll never forget they got Oscar Mayer up to dance. He thoroughly enjoyed it.

Marilyn and Bob's family

After their graduations from Stanford, Marilyn and Bob moved to New York where she was a law student at Columbia, and he was an Investment Banker with Smith Barney. Later they moved to Washington, D.C., where Bob worked in venture capital and Marilyn practiced law at Mayer, Brown and Platt, a Chicago-based firm. Later, they took a year-long sabbatical around the world. They slept in tents in the Sinai desert and visited yurts in Inner Mongolia. They spent a month in India, trekked in Nepal, drove across Kenya, saw Petra in Jordan, visited Pakistan, and spent time in Israel. After that year they moved to Chicago, and later to Madison, Wisconsin, where their first two daughters were born. They moved to Winston-Salem in 1985 when Bob joined Salem Investment Counselors, and raised their family of three daughters, Laura, Lindsay, and Ashley. They now have eight grandchildren.

Laura is married to Brendan Dugan; thier children are Bobby and Thompson.
Lindsay is married to John Grdina; their children are Blair and Alice.
Ashley is married to Brian Brooks; their children Anders, Christian, Louise, and Jonas.

Louise and Jim with Ed's family

Ed

Ed was born in 1954. He went to high school at St. James Academy but spent his senior year at Bethesda Chevy Chase High School. During that year, he often came over to the House of Representatives and volunteered to work for members of Congress. He got to know a lot of members. I distinctly remember waiting for the underground train linking the House office buildings to the Capitol, and noting that many members came and spoke to him before they spoke to me. He graduated from Wake Forest University and also earned his MBA there.

Ed has politics in his blood. He has been elected as the Republican party's national committee man for the State of North Carolina. They meet every three months and make decisions on the direction of the party. He also operates a suite of offices in Clemmons, with about 60,000 square feet. He married Melanie Pennell of Winston-Salem, and they have three children, Elizabeth, James, and Penn, and five grandchildren.

Elizabeth is married to Scott Morris; their children are Woodson, Nora Ann, and Birch.
James is married to Brittney Hagy; their children are Jameson and Brooklyn.
Penn is married to Natalie Braswell.

.

Philip

Philip was born in 1956. He loved nature, hiking, reading and painting. He was a gifted artist and won awards for some of his pieces. He attended Asheville School, started at Duke, and ended up graduating from Bentley College in the Boston area. He suffered from depression much of his adult life, but fought it bravely. He died in 2014. We miss him every day.

Philip Broyhill

An excerpt from Philip's obituary is reprinted here:

> "Philip Robbins Broyhill passed away Saturday, March 1, 2014. He was born May 16, 1956, in Lenoir, North Carolina. He graduated from The Asheville School, attended Duke University and Wake Forest University, and graduated from Bentley University in Waltham, Massachusetts. He also completed rigorous wilderness training in his youth at the National Outdoor Leadership School in Wyoming.
>
> Philip was an accomplished, award -winning, and prolific artist. He worked and exhibited in a number of studios in the Boston area over the last 30 years, and was constantly striving to reach his maximum creative potential through his paintings and pencil sketches. One of his paintings was selected for an award by the State

of Massachusetts. He had recently moved to North Carolina, where he was beginning to make his presence known in the artistic community.

In addition to his artistic gifts, Phil was blessed with a gentle and compassionate nature. He was deeply spiritual, and tried to see only good in everyone he met. He volunteered as a reader to the blind, and completed certification as a peer counselor. Philip was an avid reader and took a great interest in current events and history and served on the Board of Westbridge Community Services of Boston for a number of years."

The following is inscribed on Philip's grave:

THE ARTIST
HE WAS A QUIET GENTLE AND GENEROUS MAN
WITH A RETENTIVE AND CREATIVE MIND.
HE WAS ALWAYS A POSITIVE INFLUENCE IN THE COMMUNITY IN
WHICH HE LIVED.
HE IS NOW AT PEACE WITH HIS MAKER.

"That's the Girl for Me."

My Career at
Broyhill Furniture Industries

by Jim Broyhill

Even as a child I accompanied my parents to the furniture market in Chicago which was located on Lakeshore Drive. As a teenager I was put to work and thereby got to know the customers. I attended all the way through until I became a member of Congress. I got so I could know a customer's name, or I knew where they were from. After Chicago, I'd go to High Point, and do the same thing. This experience probably helped me in knowing my constituents later on.

Jim in business

After the war (WW II), the furniture mart building in High Point was refurbished and we got half of the top floor. One of my responsibilities was making sure we were prepared for the Market, ready to show our latest styles and so forth. I had to get the labor and get all of the samples done. There were other regions of the country that decided they wanted a furniture market — Boston, Los Angeles, Atlanta, and Dallas, and I was responsible for preparations at those markets also.

I got very much involved with building a human resources department in our company when we only had a fledgling one. I wanted to expand it, particularly in the area of training — not only for the workmen at the bench, but especially for the supervisors because we were expanding so quickly. Our supervisors needed to be firm, but they had to be fair. After work hours, we would pay the supervisors to work with professionals to learn how to manage people. I think everybody really bought into the program. We found that good leadership helped avoid discontent that might lead to unionization. We had to make sure the supervisors were treating people right, and make sure we were compensating our workforce fairly. We had three different union elections that I can remember. The employees voted "no" all three times.

I brought in specialists to promote team building. Every year, twice a year, we'd shut down the plant at noon for at least two hours — with pay — and have a sumptuous feast as well as entertainment. My father would be there, and everybody would want to shake his hand. At that time, Arthur Smith and the Crackerjacks were one of the largest country acts in America. We had him at every picnic. He'd come with me to do speeches later on, when I was in Congress. At one appearance, I gave Arthur a check to pay his fee and he sat down and wrote me the same amount for a campaign donation. I will always remember this gesture of goodwill.

J. Edgar Broyhill and the early days at Broyhill Furniture Industries

In the early 1950s, Dad called me into his office. Sitting at his desk was every furniture manufacturer in town. He told me, "We are going to build a recreation center in Lenoir, and you're going to get it started." We were able to have the city appoint a recreation board, and the manufacturers contributed funds to build the facility. Later, we also added a pool and hiking area.

Dad called me into the office on another occasion and, again, all the major furniture manufacturers were sitting around a table. Retail customers had started coming to Lenoir "pre-market" to see upcoming furniture designs. The manufacturers didn't have a place to entertain customers. The solution was the Lenoir Country Club, built in 1958 or 1959.

We showed in Chicago at the Chicago Furniture Mart in June and January. Then we would come to High Point in late January. In the early 1950s, some of the customers — particularly the department stores — wanted to get a one-up on their customers, in order to obtain something exclusive. To satisfy this demand, we set up the whole line on the second floor of the office building. Later, everything gravitated toward High Point. The June and January shows disappeared and were replaced by shows in April and October. It wasn't long after that that the Chicago market ended.

Transitioning from furniture to public service

In 1951, I had asked my best girl, Louise Robbins from Durham, to marry me. We married on June 2, the same weekend she graduated from Chapel Hill. Because Tommy Culbreath had been drafted into the Korean War and I temporarily had taken over his territory, Louise and I had to work our wedding and honeymoon plans around the dates of the Chicago and High Point summer furniture markets. After she and I were married, the company hired our friend Bruce Chester of Lenoir to take over the eastern North Carolina territory. He represented the company for many years thereafter. When Tommy returned from the war, he took over South Carolina, and he, too, remained for many years with the company.

I saw the need for a member of the family to be involved with our plants, and I became interested in the fledgling personnel program we had at the time. We were expanding fast and needed trained supervisors. Quite honestly, we were also concerned about administrative efficiency, particularly regarding order flow and inventory control.

We installed an IBM punch card system. It never worked well because of the volume of punch cards needed to account for every item we produced. We purchased another IBM system, the IBM 1401, which was the first computer on the market and probably the first to be used in the furniture business. It was an outstanding success. Through the years Broyhill continued to update and upgrade the system as new technology became available.

Brent Kincaid

In mid-August 2016, my good friend Brent Kincaid passed away. I spoke at his funeral three days later on August 18. My eulogy is printed here.

Kathryn asked me to say a few words about our dear friend, Brent, and I must be frank in saying that I was hesitant about accepting the invitation, and the reason why, as I told her, is that "I fear I will break down crying in the middle of my remarks."

Frankly, this is not the way it was supposed to be. I had Brent's name listed on my funeral plans, to give remarks at my funeral service! I always figured that if he could get me into the halls of Congress, perhaps he could get me through The Pearly Gates! Come to think about it, he now is up there on the inside, and I am hoping he is going to find a side door where I can get inside, when my time comes.

If Horatio Alger were alive today and still writing his novels, Brent Kincaid would certainly be the subject of one of those stories. In the late 1800s, Horatio Alger wrote about young men who came from humble backgrounds and rose to prominence through hard work, determination, and honesty. That is the story of the life of Brent Kincaid.

Brent and I became acquainted in the mid-1950s when he returned to Lenoir after service in the U.S. Army. Brent was teaching school and had quickly become a leader here at First Baptist Church. He was the superintendent of a group of classes, and I was one of his Sunday School teachers. In the late 1950s, I heard that Brent wanted to make a career change and had been interviewing with one or more of the furniture companies in Lenoir. I immediately called him and asked him to come and talk with me. Brent joined the company, and he began what was a fabulous career at Broyhill Furniture, ending up as President and Chief Executive Officer some 35 years later.

Just as I may have had some influence in changing Brent's life, Brent had a major influence in changing my life. In 1962, he was the campaign manager of my first and successful campaign for the U.S. Congress. I went on to win 11 more elections to that office, and he had a leadership role in each of those victories. I give credit to Brent — as well as to my wife — for getting me elected to Congress. Brent made sure that Louise had a key role in the campaign, and everywhere I took Louise on the campaign trail, people would look at her, then look back at me and then look back at her, and I could see them thinking to themselves: "Well, if SHE sees something good about this guy, maybe he is all right!"

Brent's management skills, and his organizational and motivational skills were key factors in those campaign successes. However, I often kidded Brent that he worked so hard to get me elected and to get me out of town so he could take my job!

Brent was a take-charge kind of guy. He was not bashful about expressing an opinion on a subject. If you gave him a challenge, he would do all in his power to come up with the answer. Most everyone knew this side of Brent. There was another side to Brent not as well known, and that was the countless hours he volunteered for so many worthwhile causes in the community and in the state. He served on the boards of many other community and state programs as well. For example, as a member of the N.C. Board of Transportation, he brought about the upgrading of a number of roads and highways in our area, including the two main projects to convert U.S. Highways U.S. 421 and U.S. 321 to modern, four-lane, limited access highways.

He served on the board of numerous other groups and was given many honors for this outstanding record of community service along the way.

Although Brent was not quiet about expressing his opinion on a subject, he did have a great gift for listening, and a talent for quickly coming to the central point in any question or issue you took to him.

Throughout his career he was known as a hard worker, and he was not a "yes" man. He would always give you honest advice. For example, after my first political speech, he took me aside, and said: "Jim, that speech was just awful. All you did was put people to sleep." He advised me to spice up my speeches with humorous stories in order to make a point, and that is when I became a collector of humorous stories that I could use to drive home a point.

Yes, Brent had a successful career and a well-earned retirement, but he went too soon. There are so many of his family and friends here who could tell anecdotes about the life of this good man. He was a good man. He was a good husband, a good father, and he was a good friend.

Ralph Waldo Emerson said:
> "The best and most beautiful things in the world cannot be seen, or touched, but are felt in the heart."

So, as we say goodbye to Brent, I can say that in my heart, I am thankful for those years of friendship we had, and I am thankful for all that he did for me. I will always remember him.

Flying

A friend of mine, who happened to be a neighbor and a salesman for furniture finishing materials, had a plane that he used to visit his customers, flying from Lenoir to High Point or Roanoke. I rode with him a time or two and decided to take flying lessons myself. I went to Hickory and learned how to fly. I didn't have a plane, but you could rent one in Hickory very inexpensively. Although I often flew for pleasure, much of the time I flew to High Point for business. This was back before the days of the interstate highways.

I had one close call. I left High Point and saw a weather front coming in. I immediately went to Greensboro and landed. It was a good thing I did because the front developed into a huge storm, one that I had successfully avoided. That's when I decided to give up flying. I don't think I logged more than 300 hours. Later on, the company bought aircraft and employed professional pilots. We had a Bonanza, a DC-3, and later, a Learjet.

Entry into Politics

by Jim Broyhill

I n 1948, my father was elected to represent North Carolina for the
Republican National Committee. Every state had one man and one woman.
I was 21 at the time, which was then the voting age. We traveled together
often, not only around the state but also to other areas of the country. We went
to meetings of the National Chamber of Commerce, the National Association
of Manufacturers, Republican conferences, etc. In doing so I became very well
acquainted with all the Republican leadership in our state, especially in our home
district, the old 9th District, which I would later represent in Congress.

Redistricting occurred in 1960, and North Carolina lost a Congressman, the only
time I remember that happening. In 1959, there were 12 districts. After 1960,
there were only 11, which meant some of the counties had to be added to the
remaining districts. That's what happened with our 9th district. We gained Davie
and Yadkin counties. Those are two counties that have never voted anything but
Republican since the Civil War. That made the 9th District a Republican district.

Jim and Louise Broyhill family, 1962

By late 1961, people were
calling me on the phone, asking
me to run for Congress.
I offered to help find
somebody to run. Nobody
wanted to run. There were two
prominent men that my father
and I had a lot of respect for:
I.G. Greer of Boone and
Thomasville, and Clyde R.
Green, a former mayor of
Boone and a member of the
Eisenhower administration.

Jim Broyhill enjoyed meeeting
the people he represented

Those are the two who talked me into running myself. After the first of the year, I filed as a candidate for the United States ninth congressional district, and that was it.

My bride said, "I'll let him get it out of his system. There's no way he can win." I was 35 years old, and she spent the following 24 years in Washington.

The Ninth Congressional District consisted of Caldwell, Watauga, Allegheny, Ashe, Alexander, Iredell, Rowan, Cabarrus, and Stanly counties in North Carolina. I was successful in 1962, thanks in large part to friends such as Phil Kirk and the many other volunteers who worked tirelessly on my behalf, but in the election of 1966, redistricting

removed Iredell and Alexander counties and added Avery, Wilkes, and Surry counties. In spite of the redistricting, I was reelected. Again, in 1968, the state General Assembly redistricted and placed my home county of Caldwell along with neighboring Watauga County in the 10th district, which at that time was represented by Congressman Basil Whitener, a Democrat from Gastonia. The counties in the 10th district were Gaston, Cleveland, Burke, Catawba, Caldwell, Watauga, Avery, and Alexander.

Election Victory

Notwithstanding the attempts to defeat me by redistricting, I was successful in ousting Whitener, and I beat him again in a rerun in 1970. After that, the reelection campaigns were not nearly as difficult or as expensive. All through the era of my bids for office, my brother, Paul, and my late brother-in-law Bill Stevens were most supportive and acted as my campaign fund-raisers. Because

When Jim Broyhill spoke, people listened.

of them, I never had to worry about that important part of a political campaign. My friend Brent Kincaid was the mastermind who organized the campaign strategies and implemented them, and I owe him a great debt of gratitude.

Unusual campaign strategies

I first registered to run for Congress in early February 1962. My service started Jan. 3, 1963. I immediately started to put together a campaign team. My manager was Brent Kincaid. He was a great help in planning and taking action on things that needed to be done in the campaign.

We did some unusual things that had not been done in campaigns. For example, we would get volunteers to go with us and greet the workers as they went to work. They would stand and hand out brochures to the workers who went through the gate. But a high percentage were taking a lot of those brochures and throwing them down.

Entry into Politics

About that time, Brent and I went to a campaign school in Washington sponsored by the Republican Party. I saw a member of Congress had put together a cookbook with a lot of recipes.

"I'd sure like to have this. Can I have it?"

"Sure."

When we started giving out cookbooks, people did not throw them down; they put them in their pocket to take home to Momma. We no longer had the problem of people trashing campaign information.

Plus, we organized a group of ladies to go through grocery stores handing out cookbooks. The ladies would say, "I'd like to give you a cookbook, and I'd like to introduce you to our candidate for Congress." It wasn't too long before stores said we couldn't do it anymore. Then we moved to the parking lot. They didn't seem to bother us as much then.

Capitol Cook Book
used in several campaigns

Anytime there was a parade or a county fair, we were there waving to the crowds. We handed out balloons (Louise called me "the Jolly Balloon Man.") and shook hands. Nobody had ever campaigned that way for Congress.

Meeting Phil Kirk

In 1962, I met Phil Kirk, who graciously wrote the foreword to this book.

As a senior in high school, Phil organized a lot of the teenagers into a Teenage Republican Club. They went all over Rowan County, knocking on doors. They gave out three items: a brochure on about Louise and me; a cookbook which had recipes in it from many members of Congress, and a sugar/flour scoop with my name on it. To this day, I credit Phil's efforts with my victory.

Phil went on to graduate from East Rowan High School, graduated from Catawba College, and worked his way through school by working at the Salisbury Post. He taught school in Salisbury for four and a half years, and was elected to the State Senate at age 25, while teaching and working at the Salisbury Post. At the time, he was the youngest person ever elected to the State Senate. Phil became Governor Holshouser's Chief of Staff after running the NC Department of Human Resources, now called the Department of Health and Human Services (DHHS). He became my Chief of Staff and later also Governor Martin's Chief of Staff. Phil was appointed by Governor Jim Hunt as Chairman of the N.C. Board of Education, and he also led the N.C. Chamber of Commerce.

Most importantly, Phil is a treasured friend.

Jim Broyhill with Phil Kirk
and his parents, 1978

A Friendship

Dear Phil,

Thank you, sir, for your constant care for a great and good gentleman whom you and I admire and love.

I got a call from Ed Broyhill this afternoon about his appreciation for my relationship with his dad, which uplifted me. I had to reflect on what it must mean to the Broyhill family that you have been so intensely devoted to our hero.

Yes, it was a privilege for you to have had a special position of working with Jim Broyhill. And yes, it was a privilege for him and his family to have the forever loyal presence of Phil Kirk in their life and work.

Thank you. Thank you. Thank you.

Jim Martin

Gov. Jim Martin and Sen. Jim Broyhill

Serving North Carolinians from Washington, D.C.

by Jim Broyhill

President Johnson, early Congressional days, and the growing budget

I was in Congress when the budget of the U.S. first went over $100 billion. And here we are facing trillions in spending today.

When I was freshman in the House of Representatives in 1963, I was made a member of the Republican Policy Committee. I believe I was the first freshman to be made a member of the committee. The committee was composed primarily of senior guys. It consisted of Gerald Ford and others. Charlie Halleck of Indiana was the minority leader. Ford was the conference chairman. He presided whenever all of us got together.

Jim served on the Republican Policy Committee as a freshman representative

President Kennedy wanted to cut taxes. The Republicans were concerned that cutting taxes would result in a huge deficit. When the bill came up in the House, most of the Republicans voted "no." I voted "no." The guys on the committee voted "no."

By November of 1963, Lyndon Johnson was president. He wanted to get the

Tax Bill out of the way so he could promote the Civil Rights Bill which was a priority. He was a master at parliamentary maneuvering. He knew the Senate could only tackle one issue at a time. He called all the leaders to the White House, including a very conservative senator from Virginia. Johnson asked the group "What do you want?" The response was, "Give us a budget in 1964 of under $100 billion and we will give you some votes on your tax bill. He had to get the Tax Bill through the Senate, and it would have to come back to the House to be confirmed. The bill passed both houses. That was the first time

I voted "no" initially in the House vote and then "yes" to pass the bill. The tax cuts went into effect in 1964. In January 1964, Johnson was as good as his word. He submitted a budget of $99.9 billion.

As 1964 went along, President Johnson, being the parliamentarian master, knew how the system worked. He submitted budget increases during the year called "urgent supplemental." We ended up spending $120 billion.

President Johnson

Sergeant Shriver Was Speaking My Language

Sergeant Shriver was a son-in-law of Joseph Kennedy and a brother-in-law of President Kennedy. Shriver was later a candidate for vice president, in 1972. Joseph Kennedy owned the Chicago Merchandise Mart, which at one time was the largest building in America. He wanted a furniture market to be held at the Merchandise Mart and came to Lenoir on one occasion to discuss this.

When I went to Congress, Shriver was head of the Peace Corps. One of the first bills I had to consider was the reauthorization of the Peace Corps. Shriver came into my office trying to get votes to support reauthorization. He used a furniture term to get my vote. "When you have a successful furniture group, you authorize a new cutting," he said. "I want you to authorize a new cutting for this program."

The Death of President Kennedy

I was playing golf at the Congressional Country Club on Nov. 22, 1963. We had no session that day. We were on number 9, putting out, and somebody yelled out, "They shot the President in Dallas!" I immediately ran to the locker room, changed clothes, and went to my office. My staff had already prepared my remarks. I had a great chief of staff, Vince Monzell, and was grateful that he had taken care of that in advance. Then all of the preparations began for the funeral service. Everybody knows the story of how Jacqueline took the lead on this, and that she had the funeral service designed to be similar to that of President Lincoln's.

JFK Funeral Procession

The decision was made to inter Kennedy in Arlington and have an eternal flame by the grave. Congressional members and their wives were brought to Arlington for the graveside service. Despite the fact that this was my first year in Congress and in general freshman congressmen are seen and not heard, on that particular occasion, Louise and I were given seats in the front row, close to the Kennedy family. We were able to witness the lighting of the flame and watch as dignitaries came to be seated. Most memorable was Charles DeGaulle, president of France, extremely tall at 6 feet 5 inches, followed by Halle Selasse, emperor of Ethiopia, who was only 5 feet 2 inches tall.

Dick Nixon

My father was chairman of the Republican National Committee in North Carolina. As a member of that committee, he got acquainted with all the Republican leaders.

In 1948, I went to the National Convention in Philadelphia with him and was introduced to these leaders.

Dick Nixon became vice president in 1953 under President Dwight D. Eisenhower and served until 1961. My first meeting with Nixon was around 1956 or 1957. A year or so before, I'd bought a piece of property in Lenoir I wanted to build my house on. It was on the site of an old golf course and had a beautiful view. Our cousin, Marvin T. Broyhill, who was in the homebuilding business in Washington, took us on a ride in Washington to see architectural styles. I hadn't hired an architect yet but wanted to get some ideas of styles we liked. As we went by one house in Cleveland Park, we saw Dick Nixon, the Vice President of the United States, out in the front yard mowing the grass.

Jim met Richard Nixon long before he became President.

In 1958, Nixon made a diplomatic trip to South America. While he was in Peru, the Peruvians were agitated by the far left to almost assassinate him. The Secret Service was able to get him out of the mob, but it was a very scary time. Soon after that, he came to our hometown, Lenoir, and to Blowing Rock, where he was making a speech. My father held a really nice reception for him at the old Mayview Manor Hotel in Blowing Rock. I've got a picture of that. I was there, but I'm not in the photo.

> "We saw Dick Nixon, the Vice President of the United States, out in the front yard mowing the grass."

We had a summer home nearby, and Dick Nixon came to the house and spent a good part of the afternoon, relaxing and napping and so forth. We took him to the hotel, about 700 or 800 yards away, for the reception. People came from all over to see him. After that, he ran for governor of California but was not elected. He moved to New York and became a partner in a law firm, Nixon, Mudge, Rose, Guthrie and Alexander.

In 1964, when he was practicing law in New York, one of his law partners was a member of the Board of Trustees of Pfeiffer College, which later became Pfeiffer University. He made the arrangements for Nixon to come to Pfeiffer to make remarks on foreign affairs. Pfeiffer was in my congressional district. I immediately called Dick and said, "I'd like to ask you to do something for me while you're here. Would you speak at a fundraiser for me?"

He said, "I'm just not doing that right now. What about a reception?"

"Well, I'd be delighted to arrange a reception," I replied, adding "but I'll have to put out an invitation."

Then I got a call from Arthur Smith. "I understand Dick Nixon is coming to Pfeiffer," he said. "I wonder if you could arrange for him to be on my program."

"I'll do my best," I said.

Arthur Smith had the largest country western program in America. It originated at WBTV Channel 3 in Charlotte, North Carolina, and ran all over the country in syndication.

I called Nixon and said, "I would strongly recommend that you do this. It will take us an hour to get to Charlotte, an hour on the program and an hour back. It will take three hours of your time, and it will be shown all over America."

The Arthur Smith Show from Charlotte was the largest country & western music program in America.

So, we did it. We got a Highway Patrolman to take us down there. Dick Nixon did a marvelous job. He did a little interview and he played a song or two on the piano.

The reception was at the old National Armory in Salisbury. At the appointed time, I picked him up from the old Howard Johnson's in Salisbury. We got there about five minutes early and there were a few people milling around outside. I thought, "This isn't a very good turnout." Then I realized the reason for the people outside the event venue: they couldn't get inside. Inside, the place was packed with people! There must have been 1,000 people there. I'm not kidding you.

We'd fixed up two platforms. We had a platform where Louise and I and Dick Nixon stood. People could come up on that platform and shake hands. Across from that, I had photographers on the other platform, taking pictures while we were shaking hands.

At some point, I asked him, "You wanna quit?"

He said, "No, I want to shake hands with all of them."
He made some remarks, and then we went to the Salisbury airport and took our family plane to Washington National. We got off, and the plane took him on

to New York. Here was a man not even in office, but I'll bet you pictures from that event are still on mantelpieces.

In 1964, all the Republicans were facing a bad year, and we needed all the help we could get. The Democrats had ended up with a 2-to-1 majority. We held a rally at 9 a.m. at Catawba College. By 8:30 a.m., it was packed. That's how popular Dick Nixon was. But, of course, we lost that election, and Lyndon Johnson won by a landslide. Four years later, Johnson was so unpopular because of Vietnam that he refused to run for another term.

Jim with President Nixon

Dick Nixon was elected president in the 1968 election. During his presidency, he invited Louise and me to the White House often. I must confess I never saw the "dark side" of Dick Nixon until shortly before he resigned. It made me very, very depressed and disappointed that he had those flaws and that personality. And I was disappointed in myself for not seeing it.

During the Vietnam War and all the protests, Nixon did not try to go to church as Johnson had done. He started holding services in the White House in the grand ballroom, and our family was invited.

> "**I** must confess I never saw the "dark side" of Dick Nixon until shortly before he resigned."

Over the years we were invited to many Embassy and White House dinner parties during Nixon's and other administrations. Among the most memorable were state dinners with the Shah of Iran and the king and queen of Spain, and a backyard barbeque at the White House with Nancy and Ron Reagan. I was in the Oval Office often.

When Johnson became president, Louise danced with him at a White House dinner. One of the good-looking officers on his staff came up and asked her to dance. Then he asked her, "Would you like to dance with the president?" He handed Louise to President Johnson, then another staff member came up to dance with Louise and he took her back to the table with me.

The last time I saw Dick Nixon was when he came to Winston-Salem in January 1989. He did a fundraiser for Governor Jim Martin, who had been elected governor in 1984 and was re-elected in 1988. (Martin was elected to the House in 1973 and served six terms until 1985.) You'd be surprised at how many people came out to have their picture taken with Nixon. He'd been through a major scandal but was still very popular.

> **"I'd rather be met by his pretty blonde wife."**

When arrangements were being made for his visit in 1989 to support Governor Jim Martin, I was asked to meet Nixon at the Winston-Salem airport and take him to the first event. When told of the arrangements, here are Dick Nixon's exact words: "I'd rather be met by his pretty blonde wife." So Louise accompanied me to the airport.

That was the last time I saw him. He died on April 22, 1994. I felt like he tried at the end to become a little less dogmatic, more willing to listen, and more diplomatic. Nevertheless, because of 1974, Republicans were defeated badly across the board, ending with the Congress 2 to 1 in favor of Democrats. Dick Nixon was blamed for that. Because of Nixon, a number of people went to jail and a large number of people lost their seats in Congress around the country. Many Americans lost trust in their leaders and institutions.

It was hard to forgive.

Both Nixon and Martin were members of a group called "The Chowder and Marching Club." My club was "SOS" — "Society of Statesmen," and a third group

Jim and Louise meeting
President Nixon in earlier days

was the "Acorns." Once a week, the groups would gather separately in someone's office. The routine was to go around the room taking turns discussing the activities of our respective committees. Thus, we were able to communicate informally with each other about what was going on and anticipate major legislation that was coming up. Nixon wrote about his charter membership in the "Chowder and Marching Club": "All of us were young, all of us were new members of Congress. All of us were veterans of World War II. We were concerned about the strength of the United States, and we were concerned about how we could help secure peace."

The Attempt to Cite CBS
for Being in Contempt of Congress

This is a story from the Vietnam War days. The war in Vietnam was heating up. Richard Nixon had won the presidency, with pledges to bring the war to a conclusion. However, the war was escalating and not going well.

CBS, the television giant, ran a series of stories about the war, and the story became rather controversial in that it was critical of the Pentagon's handling of the war, noting the thousands of lives lost and billions of dollars expended with no apparent gain.

Harley Staggers of West Virginia was Chairman of my Committee, the Interstate and Foreign Commerce Committee. He was also Chair of the Investigation Subcommittee which for years was regularly poking around in various agencies that had some relationship with the legislative jurisdiction of the committee. Since the committee had jurisdiction over communications and the Federal Communications Act, Chairman Staggers was concerned about the charges being made. He maintained that CBS was responsible for what today is termed "fake news."

Frank Stanton, President of CBS, was called before the subcommittee and testified that the program was fairly done, and that the conclusions were accurate. When Chairman Staggers ordered him to submit to the committee all the "outtakes" — that is, all other material filmed that was not used in the final version of the program that was narrated and run by Roger Mudd — he refused to do so, citing freedom of the press under the First Amendment to the Constitution. Chairman Staggers, and the majority on the subcommittee, immediately threatened him with a citation for Contempt of Congress for not complying with a request for and by Congress for information.

The Contempt of Congress citation came before the full committee for a vote. This effort gave me a great deal of unease. On the one hand, I was in favor of fair coverage of the subject matter by CBS and Roger Mudd. At the same time, I had grave concerns that the committee was attempting to bully one of the major television and news networks into revising their coverage of current events. In my mind this was going too far in carrying out our legislative responsibility. Also, this action came on the heels of a similar action that

Chairman Staggers had made in a controversy with the chairman of the Federal Communications Committee.

Staggers had previously asked the committee to cite the FCC chairman for Contempt of Congress for not turning over material the commission had legally gathered in its legislatively granted procedure to write a certain regulation pertaining to use of the airwaves. Congress had an established custom of delegating rulemaking authority to independent agencies to regulate certain areas of the economy, but the agency findings were not disclosed to the public until after the agency had completed its work. Only then was the entire record open for review. This was to protect the agency in its deliberations from political pressure, or pressure from Congress. The FCC chairman said in effect: "We have not completed our work. If the Congress wants a certain outcome on this issue, then the correct procedure is to pass a law, a law that involves the entire Congress in the decision, not just a few on one committee of one chamber of Congress. We will complete our work and then turn over to Congress the entire record of our work."

It just so happened that the citation for Contempt of Congress involving the FCC had been voted on by the committee on the very day that the FCC chairman was retiring after a long career with the agency. I thought Chairman Staggers had been wrong about the FCC matter, and I believed he was going too far in the CBS case, notwithstanding what anyone may have thought about how the subject matter was handled. So I voted "no" along with a few other members of my committee.

All of this occurred late in the afternoon, and I trudged back to my office, trying to think of how in the world I was going to deal with this issue. I was the senior member on the minority side who voted "no," so I had the responsibility of writing out my views and getting others to sign it for inclusion in the committee report. Also, I would have to plan my appearance at the Rules Committee, which acts as the "traffic cop" on all legislation. It determines the rules of debate in the House, controls the time, and decides whether amendments are in order or not. In other words, I had to come up with an overall plan of how to deal with this issue.

As I came back into my office, who should be seated in the staff room but James Srodes. He had been the press aide to Congressman Nick Galifianakis of North Carolina and was then writing for *Business Week* magazine. James was also a former reporter for the *Durham* (N.C.) *Herald*, and he was marriied to my very able legislative assistant Cecile. I told Jim what was going on, and what my immediate problem was: to write a minority view and sign it without delay; to get my views printed within the Committee Report; and most importantly, to circulate them to all members as quickly as possible. This issue was going to hit the morning news big time, and I wanted something on members' desks early the next morning. It was imperative that my colleagues could see there was another side to the story and, above all, that there were members who were not only opposed to citing CBS for Contempt of Congress, but also willing to stand up and voice those objections.

Jim Srodes said, "Let me help you get something on paper." I replied that I would be most grateful if he would do that for me. He sat down at a typewriter and in about 20 minutes had written the most elegant and articulate argument against taking the Contempt action that anyone could have written. In the meantime, I was calling Members and got several who agreed to sign the minority views.

Jim was there at the right time and had the masterful talent for words that I did not possess. The beautifully crafted piece that he wrote on my behalf was printed prominently in the Committee Report and we were able to circulate those views to all House members in a timely manner.

Business Abroad

Bringing Home a Constituent's Son from Vietnam

Sometime in the late 1960s or early 1970s, I was in Kinston preparing to give a speech. Before I was introduced, a man with the last name of Craig stood up from the audience and said, "I want to tell the audience what this man did to save my life. I had a death in the family and couldn't get a compassionate leave. Two hours after I was told I could not go, a helicopter landed in the boondocks of Vietnam, under orders from Congressman Broyhill. Forty-eight hours later, I was home. I heard later the area I'd been in was overrun by Viet Cong."

That was the best introduction I've ever had. I was given the credit, but in all honesty the help I was able to give to my constituents was in large part due to my fantastic staff.

"Please keep our son safe."

One day a man and woman came to the office; their son, who was in uniform, was with them. This was their only son, and he was on his way

> **"One of the roles of being a Congressman is being an ombudsman, helping people solve problems through their government."**

to Vietnam. They were concerned about what kind of danger he'd be in. I called the colonel of the liaison office to come up. He checked his orders. The man had been trained to use sophisticated office equipment.

"Your son will never encounter a bullet fired in anger," the colonel told the young man's parents. "However, there is a shortage of people who can operate this equipment and your son is needed in Vietnam."

About two or three weeks later, the colonel came to see me and said, "I thought you'd like to know what happened to our young man. He got off the plane in Saigon and was immediately transported to another outpost. His superior handed him an M-16 and told him they were under attack."

Fortunately, he got home all right.

One of the roles of being a Congressman is being an ombudsman, helping people solve problems through their government. We called that casework. It is one of the roles that has grown greatly in the last several decades. Examples are Social Security disability, veterans benefits, and so forth. We had an enormous amount of casework, and the war compounded that. I was fortunate that my competent and efficient staff accomplished so much, so well, for my constituents, which was a priority for me.

Are we still fighting King George?

Back in the 1970s, we had an energy shortage when Saudi Arabia and other OPEC nations cut back on delivery of crude oil and refined petroleum products to the U.S. I was on the Energy and Commerce Committee as the senior Republican. I had a request for a meeting with a group of MP's [Member of Parliament] from the British House of Commons to talk about energy. On their visit we did discuss energy for a short while, but got on the subject of the differences between the way the U.S. House works, that is totally different from the way the House of Commons works. I even took the group over to the House Floor, which is open to nonmembers when the House is not in session.

I explained our system of "checks and balances." The Congress passes

Serving North Carolinians from Washington, D.C.

legislation, and the President can sign it or veto it. The Congress then has power to override a Presidential veto. We talked about how I as a Republican could vote differently from my GOP leadership or differently from the then GOP President, and as long as the people in my district are happy with me, I can stay in office as long as I want. But the bottom line is that under the system of "checks and balances," history has shown that at certain times the Congress has the most power, and at other times, the President is predominant.

About this time, one of the MP's spoke up and said: "By Jove, you chaps are still fighting King George!!!" So, whenever you hear and read about conflicts between the White House and the Congress, and nothing gets done, it is because, as the fellow said, we are "still fighting King George!"

Vietnam — Congressional delegation to search for MIAs

There was a well-liked and well-known Congressman by the name of Gillespie V. "Sonny" Montgomery. He was from Mississippi. He was asked by the Speaker to organize a special committee to go to Vietnam to check to see if there were any remaining POWs and MIAs. This was about 1979.

This particular trip was the first official visit by Americans to Vietnam. Our trips were CODEL, they call them, Congressional Delegations.

We flew out of Andrews Air Force Base with short stops on the way over in Hawaii and the Philippines.

We landed in Hanoi, where we were guests of the Vietnamese nation. We were taken to the center of Hanoi and put into the finest hotel. There weren't that many rooms, but enough for our group, and a beautiful dining hall. The top people from their administration stayed with us and had lunch with us.

We had a visit with the president of Vietnam and we met with Gen. Giap, who led all the North Vietnamese forces. He was asking at that time for a trade relationship with the United States. We did not grant any trade relationship for a few more years, but a good part of the furniture that's marketed today is made in Vietnam.

We traveled to Laos, a poor country. When I went out to the front of hotel, there in the yard were several water buffalo. In Laos, the national government cooperated with us. They had found several bodies of American MIAs. We contacted the office in Hawaii to identify the remains. We had a ceremony when we delivered the remains to the planes.

Congressional Delegation to Russia – 1982

Bob Dole called me a day or so after the election of 1982 and said that he was getting up a delegation to attend a US/ USSR trade conference to be held in Moscow. It would include top businessmen in America and all the top USSR trade officials. We would be the guests of the Central Committee. He said that Elizabeth would be a part of the CoDel (Congressional Delegation) and wanted Louise to be a part of the group as well. As I recall, we departed a week before Thanksgiving. It so happened that Leonid Brezhnev died at that time, and the state funeral services for him were held the day we arrived. As our motorcade entered the city from the airport, we passed VP George H.W. Bush's motorcade leaving the city for the airport for his return trip to the U.S.

Jim and Louise with Bob and Elizabeth Dole at the Bolshoi Ballet

We had other members in the CoDel. I recall Congressman John Breaux of Louisiana and Congressman and Mrs. Bill Frenzel of Minnesota. Also on board the aircraft were a number of leading US businessmen such as Whitney McMillan of Cargil and Dwayne Andrus of ADM (Archer-Daniels-Midland), plus leaders of leading farm organizations.

A number of meetings were held at the hotel and in the Kremlin with various speeches, remarks, etc. Elizabeth Dole was invited to speak at one of the luncheons. At the time she was Director of the Office of Public Liaison for President Reagan. Bob and I and our wives were invited to lay a wreath at the grave site of Brezhnev, which we did.

Elizabeth is from Salisbury, North Carolina, and I mentored her when she first came to Washington; she remains a good friend. Bob was a longstanding friend and we talked by phone regularly until his recent death in late 2021.

That evening in Moscow, we were invited to the Bolshoi, guests of the Central Committee, for a performance of *Swan Lake*. We were given the courtesy of VIP box seats.

Elizabeth Dole Campaigning for Jim in North Carolina, 1986

Serving North Carolinians from Washington, D.C.

53

As the CoDel continued we visited Geneva where we celebrated Thanksgiving and also visited Bonn, Cologne, and Paris. Along the way we had many conferences and visits with various economic groups, Ambassadors, and top Swiss, German, and French officials.

Are you Congressman Broyhill?"

While in Moscow, I got the strangest request I'd ever received. Bob Dole, Elizabeth Dole, Louise, and I were standing in Red Square. We had just come from the Bolshoi Ballet's performance of Swan Lake.

Somebody tapped me on the shoulder and said, "Are you not Congressman Broyhill?"

I said, "Yes. Who are you?"

"We are a TV crew from WRAL in Raleigh and we're here on a People to People visit. But when we came into the country this morning, officials confiscated our cameras. Can you get them back for us?"

Had I been in Washington, I'd have known how to accomplish this. But it would be more complicated in Moscow. What follows is how I got their equipment back, by the next day, in Moscow.

Bob was the leader of the delegation, and I was the #2 man. The next morning, we had breakfast with the members of the Central Committee, the group right under Chairman Yuri Andropov, who held the position in Russia that Putin holds today. We had a good meeting going. Bob rose to say how delighted we were to be there. The Russians were voicing the same pleasantries. Then Bob turned and recognized me.

I got up and said my thank yous. But then I told them what happened the night before. I told them there was a group of people here from North Carolina and when they came into the country their cameras were confiscated. I said, "What will the headlines in the United States be tomorrow? The story will be about American cameras being confiscated and will not mention the good trade relations developing between our two countries." Immediately men from the Russian delegation jumped up and went over to the corner to talk.

The Raleigh group got their cameras back that day.

We had meetings with the top officers of Russia except Andropov. He was not well. In fact, he did not live too long after that. He served from November 10, 1982, upon the death of Leonid Brezhnev, until his own death on February 9, 1984.

A Champion of Constituent Service

by Mary Trimble

Senator James Broyhill had an excellent reputation for constituent service work, the focus of which included Armed Services matters, the Department of Veterans Affairs, Social Security Administration claims, State Department issues (passports and visas), and miscellaneous problems with various other federal agencies. Among other Members of Congress and across Federal agencies, Senator Broyhill was considered a champion of constituent services.

The 10th Congressional District of North Carolina consisted of many counties over the years. Congressman Broyhill had three district offices, as central as possible, so any constituent could easily come by as well as call. These offices were staffed by employed constituents who were sympathetic, energic, and committed to serving the 10th Congressional District on Congressman Broyhill's behalf. On occasion, a motorhome was rented so he could travel throughout the entire district, even to more remote areas.

Constituents came in droves, the lines were long, but Congressman Broyhill personally saw everyone who came. Most inquiries during these personal visits were constituent service problems and the staff went to work on whatever the problems might be. There were tears of joy and tears of sorrow during these visits. But many individuals came just to personally meet him, extend their thanks, express opinions, or simply shake his hand.

Congressman Broyhill insisted that each of his constituents, with whatever problems they brought to his attention, were given every consideration, in a reasonable amount of time. Unfortunately, not all issues could be favorably resolved because of the law or regulations. The staff always sent a letter and follow-ups if necessary. Every situation was thoroughly researched and reviewed. When our review uncovered a mistake in the claim or we could help with their admission to a VA Hospital or to a military assignment, Congressman Broyhill always tried to call the constituent personally with a favorable report. We also made sure that applications for benefits, or whatever the situation, received every consideration by his office and the agency involved. The Congressman's interest in the claim or the person's circumstances remained a matter of record and the office would be advised as the adjudication process continued until a final decision was made.

The times when someone's problems with the military, the VA, or Social Security Administration uncovered a mistake in the law, the Congressman would introduce legislation to correct the inequality, if appropriate. A good example occurred during the war in Vietnam. A sole surviving son was defined as the only remaining son in a family who lost a father or son during combat or who became permanently and totally disabled because of military service. A sole surviving son, not only son, was not sent into a war zone. What about a family that had one or more than one son and was being sent into combat involuntarily? (There was still a draft then.) The Congressman was confronted with this issue. He did not believe a parent should have to worry or fear another son in a combat zone if his brother or father was killed or severely disabled from the service. He introduced a bill to correct this situation and this inequity in the law. His amendment passed the House of Representatives, went on to the Senate, and became law. No servicemember from then forward was forced into a combat zone involuntarily if he had a sibling or parent that was killed in a combat zone or ruled permanently and totally disabled from military service. This is just one situation where constituent service work showed inequity in the law and Congressman Broyhill successfully corrected it. No family from then on anywhere in the country had that worry during the war in Vietnam.

The majority of Vietnam Prisoners of War (POWs) were returned from North Vietnam in February 1973. Several of these men were from the 10th Congressional District. Congressman Broyhill and staff anxiously watched as these brave Americans came down the steps of the airplane to greet their families. Many had not seen their loved ones in years. Over ten years later, the Congress decided to award the next of kin of those still listed as missing in action (MIA) honorary medals posthumously, as a keepsake. If the MIA serviceman listed North Carolina as their home of record, their next of kin (many children by then were adults) were honored and awarded this medal. North Carolina was the first state to hold such a ceremony. As the dean of the delegation (that Member of Congress having the most seniority in each state), Congressman Broyhill was given the privilege to hold the honorary ceremony. It was held at Seymour Johnson Air Force Base with the entire NC delegation present. The ceremony included speeches, remarks by several former POWs, the awarding of the medals, and a missing-man-formation flyover. This was a powerful and memorable experience for all who attended. As a result, many Congressional offices called the Congressman for guidelines on how to put together and host such an impactful event. Senator Broyhill always held first class events and this ceremony was certainly a fitting and proper tribute to these brave American heroes and their families.

Congressman Broyhill had a legacy among his colleagues and government agencies for outstanding constituent service. If there were any inequities in laws or regulations, he and his staff would get to the root of the problem. Because of this, people from other districts were always calling on him to help them. It was necessary for our office to send their inquiries to their own Congressman. There was a longstanding custom in Congress to allow every Member the opportunity to serve the constituents he represented.

Senator Broyhill remained humble. His staff always admired and respected him. Many worked for him for many years, which was not always the case on Capitol Hill. We all were hard working and loyal and remained close friends with him and his family for his lifetime. Senator Broyhill was a joy to work for and with. Every staff member who worked for him over his many years of service considered it a privilege and a blessing to do so.

Reliable Constituent Service

As a Congressman, Jim Broyhill was noted especially for his constituent service. Some requests were especially memorable, this one recalled by Cecile Srodes from the 1969 inauguration of President Richard Nixon.

A few days before the inauguration, Congressman Broyhill's Administrative Assistant, Vince Monzel, got a request for help from an assistant to Reverend Billy Graham. Vince and the assistant knew one another. Billy Graham was bringing a group of 40 people to the inauguration, and a member of Nixon's staff, Jeb Stuart Magruder, had promised them tickets. He did not deliver on that promise, so Graham's office called on the Broyhill office for help. Everyone in the office pitched in and worked the phones like telemarketers, calling other Congressional offices for extra tickets. We succeeded and secured tickets for the whole group, including a seat for the celebrated Ethel Waters, who was then in a wheelchair. After the inauguration, Billy Graham sent a stack of Bibles to the office as a thank-you.

Rev. Billy Graham and Jim Broyhill at the U.S. Capitol, likely recalling in their conversation the Congressman's earlier help in getting tickets to the 1969 Presidential Inauguration. (undated photo)

—Cecile Srodes

Hugh Morton and Grandfather Mountain

In the mid-1960s the National Park Service wanted to route the Blue Ridge Parkway over the top of Grandfather Mountain. Hugh Morton opposed this as it would have ruined the natural beauty of the mountain which he had worked so hard to preserve. I worked with other members of the North Carolina Delegation to persuade NPS to use the parkway route we travel today. Hugh was an ardent Democrat, but after we worked together on preserving Grandfather Mountain, we became good friends.

Jim Broyhill (left) and Hugh Morton (right)
(unidentified person, center)

(l to r) U.S. Senator Sam Ervin, Gov. Dan Moore, Art Director for NPS Bill Horton, Rep. Jim Broyhill, BRP Assoc. President Ronaold Ligon, BRP Superintendent Granville Liles gather in breaking ground for the Blue Ridge Parkway alignment to avoid Grandfather Mountain.

North Carolina
Secretary of Commerce
by Jim Broyhill

I served as North Carolina Secretary of Commerce under Governor Jim Martin who served from 1985 to 1993. Here is how that came about.

In 1986 when John East, who was one of North Carolina's U.S. Senators, decided not to run for another term, I decided to run for Senate. I had served continually in the House of Representatives since being elected in 1962. With 24 years of experience serving the citizens of North Carolina in Congress, having me

Gov. Jim Martin with Senator Broyhill

continue that service as a Senator would be good for North Carolina. David Funderburk opposed me in a primary in May, and I defeated him quite decisively. Then the race was between former Governor Terry Sanford and me. I ran on a platform supporting Reagan's policies, which polls showed were popular. During the campaign, Senator East died from suicide. On June 29, Governor Martin appointed me to fill that seat in the Senate for the remainder of the term.

The race was expensive. In my first campaign, we spent less than $100,000. But in the Senate campaign we spent $10 million. I think my opponent spent a little more than I did. For comparison, Ted Budd spent $100 million in his recent

2022 campaign. My 1986 campaign would have been about a fourth of that at $27 million today.)

Governor Sanford defeated me in November 1986 and immediately took the Senate seat.

I quickly became a part of North Carolina economic development efforts. Governor Martin named me as Chairman of the N.C. Board of Economic Development. Our board met quarterly around the state, hearing from various leaders from private and government sectors. In our day-long meetings, we discussed plans to build the state's economy. Soon enough, I was also serving as the acting Secretary of Commerce because the actual Secretary was ill. When he was unable to continue in that role and soon retired, the governor asked me to replace him.

Commerce Secretary Broyhill and Gov. Jim Martin with Andy Griffith, who sang in Glee Club with Senator Broyhill at UNC-Chapel Hill

During his time as Commerce Secretary, Jim and Gov. Jim Martin went to Hollywood to explore the film-making industry opportunites for North Carolina. Andy Griffith welcomed them and gave them a tour as they were driven around town in his convertible.

The North Carolina Commerce Department has a vital role in several areas to help build the state's economy. It fosters new and expanding businesses and industries; works with foreign affairs to help North Carolina companies do business in other countries; and, it has a division to attract moviemakers to North Carolina.

To promote North Carolina business in foreign companies I traveled to various countries in Europe, as well as to Japan and to Seoul, South Korea. We visited with companies which were expanding to the United States. We wanted to tell them about the opportunities we had in North Carolina, and we had some great victories. I am proud that at that time, North Carolina was #1 in the United States for attracting new industries.

One of the tasks handed to me was to develop a sister relationship with Taiwan. The Taiwanese asked us to visit and hosted our delegation at a dinner which included a long ceremony and some speeches, followed by numerous toasts with a powerful alcoholic libation. After the dinner was over, my staff member, who spoke Chinese, came over to me and said, "I just thought you would want to know that our hosts are a little bit angry with you."

"What did I do?" I asked.

My aide confided, "He saw that you put aside the toasting cocktail and drank Coca-Cola."

But my aide was quick on his feet because he told them, "The Secretary is a Baptist."

The truth was that despite being Baptist, I was not opposed to an occasional cocktail or wine, but I had not realized that by declining the local strong concoction I had possibly given offense. The explanation my aide gave to them saved the day and mollified the Taiwanese at the banquet.

Remembering Senator Broyhill at the
N.C. Department of Commerce

by Ernie Pearson

I came to the Department of Commerce as the Assistant Secretary for Finance and Administration one month prior to Senator Broyhill joining the Department on February 1, 1989. I later assumed the role of Assistant Secretary of Economic Development, so I worked with the Senator extensively throughout his tenure.

Senator Broyhill succeeded Claude Pope who resigned for health reasons. The Senator came to this role from being Chairman of the North Carolina Board of Economic Development.

As Secretary of Commerce, the Senator oversaw several divisions: Business Industry, Travel and Tourism, International Trade Division, Film Industry Promotion, and Commerce Finance. More divisions and responsibilities were added during his tenure.

Immediately the Department implemented one of the most innovative State programs in the country, a retention and expansion program for existing industry. To our knowledge, North Carolina was the first State ever to implement this type of program. Senator Broyhill was involved in making it highly successful. Additionally, he made it a practice to call on companies which were already operating in the State as a statement of our commitment to the industry. I learned from the Senator the value of getting out into the field with staff making these existing industry calls. This was similar to what the Senator did so well when he was a Congressman.

The Senator made it clear that his interest was in being the outward facing representative of the State and the Department of Commerce. He depended upon staff to handle management functions and details, although he was always aware of the status of those matters. One of his strengths was that he had good people working for him and he let them run the programs without micromanaging them.

Early on, the Senator thought it would be good to visit with the Commissioner of Agriculture, Jim Graham. I attended this meeting and we discussed ways we might cooperate with the Department of Agriculture and their work regarding overseas markets and recruitment of companies in the agricultural industry. The Senator suggested that our two departments should meet quarterly to coordinate. I was told later by someone who was also in the meeting that after we left the room, Commissioner Graham just stared at the door to his office for quite a while. Then he turned to his senior staff and said, "That's the smartest damn Republican I have ever met. He's the only Secretary of Commerce who has ever come to my office to talk with me about cooperating on economic development efforts." When I related this to the Senator, he laughed heartily. We both were absolutely surprised that no Secretary of Commerce had ever shown the courtesy of going to meet with the Commissioner of Agriculture to discuss these matters. That visit helped forge a great working relationship with Jim Graham, a Democrat, that lasted throughout Senator Broyhill's tenure.

Even during contentious politics between the Democratic legislature and the Republican governor's administration, Senator Broyhill worked to reestablish contact on a cooperative basis. Certainly, his reputation working across partisan lines helped in that regard. I noted with interest that many times we would go to meet with legislators, whose offices in the Legislative Building were very small. They would have a desk, a desk chair and then two visitors' chairs crammed into a very small space. But they were very respectful of the Senator. I cannot count the number of times that I saw legislators get up and ask Secretary Broyhill to take their seat in the desk chair, and they would come around and sit in one of the other chairs for a discussion.

Our department's efforts in this Session and future ones were very successful. We won every appropriation and program request that we sought, with the exception of one. We defeated everything we opposed.

In Congress, the Senator was used to committee meetings being planned well ahead of time, the topics being known, and allowing for the preparation of information to be presented. This is not how it worked in the North Carolina General Assembly. But Senator Broyhill adapted to the process and was an extraordinarily successful spokesman for the Department of Commerce.

NC Secretary of Commerce

He started the process and the relationship that carried over to a long-term positive relationship between the Department and the Legislature during the last four years of Governor Martin's term.

We soon turned our attention to projecting Senator Broyhill out into the field in marketing efforts to promote North Carolina. These marketing efforts required numerous trips around the United States, in Canada, all over Europe and through Asia. This was a demanding agenda. Recruitment trips to Asia and Europe would last two weeks with calls back-to-back throughout the weekdays. Senator Broyhill was highly effective in these marketing efforts.

Those of us who worked with the Senator during those years recall the experience with pleasure and a sense of accomplishment under his leadership and notably how wonderful he was to work with. I am sure the Senator would not take credit for all of this, but during his tenure the Department of Commerce accomplished these notable successes:

-Creation of the Sports Development Program, instrumental in bringing the US Open to North Carolina in 1994.

-Creation of the first-ever state level existing industry program.

-Recognition on several occasions as having one of the top recruitment efforts and winning the Governor's Cup Award, recognition by Site Selection Magazine for winning the most large projects.

-Leading the nation on more than one occasion during his tenure in recruiting international companies.

-Leading the nation during his tenure in recruiting research and development projects.

-Being recognized each year of his tenure by Site Selection Magazine as one of the top ten economic development business recruitment programs in the Country, and the only State program so listed.

It was my honor to work with Senator Broyhill during his service as Secretary of Commerce for North Carolina.

"The Naked Truth"

Reflections by Alvah Ward

I served nearly 30 years in the Commerce Department and in many other roles, from Seafood Industry Consultant to Industrial Developer to Director of the Business/Industry Development Division, and finally Director of Marketing for the Global Transpark, before retiring in 1995. During this entire period, I can honestly say Senator Broyhill was the most honorable and effective boss I ever had. He was an effective leader who encouraged excellence, rejected criticism of others, and was quick to offer praise for good work.

He also had a wonderful sense of humor. I offer two examples. I always tried to arrive for work around 15-30 minutes early each day. One morning when I arrived early, I had a note pinned to the post near my parking place. It read "WHAT KEPT YOU?" When I found him, he was in the coffee shop with "the boys."

As Director of the Business and Industry Division of the Department, I had the responsibility for recruiting industries to North Carolina. A group of people wanted to start a nudist colony in the state and called my office. I merely had my staff send some literature from the state to the person who called me. Not long after, I had an urgent call to report to the Secretary's office. I had not the slightest notion what this was all about. On arrival I was told that a very important meeting was being held to announce that I had been awarded Secretary Broyhill's "Balance Growth Award." With a great deal of pomp and circumstance, I was presented with a framed clipping from the Northhampton County Times. It read as follows: "We are happy to announce the location of our first nudist colony in North Carolina. This would not have been possible without the tremendous support we have received from Mr. Alvah Ward of the North Carolina Department of Commerce."

Statesmanship

Broyhill Staff

I have been extremely fortunate over the years to have had people working on my staff and volunteering on my campaigns who have contributed to my success, enriched my life, and made me look good! I have tried to list everyone here, but there are many others. I am profoundly grateful to all.

2007 reunion

Alicia _____	Rita Castle	Nan Ellwood
Austin Allran	Tami Diener Chodak	Lisa Foley
Gail Ayers	Barbara Clements	Rob Foreman
Nancy Barnes Benford	Susan Asmus Cobb	Debbie French
Lisa Black	Sue Shuster Comers	Mary Ann Ganey
Betty Conley Bourie	Betty Conley	Gloria Gardner
John Briar	Diane Cook	Jayne Gillenwaters
Kevin Brown	Elizabeth Danforth	Diane Goodwin
Rebecca Williams Brown	Gail Davies	Nell Guffey
Sandy Burke	Wilma Dawson	Sandy Gumerove

Drew Hiatt
Jo Ann Hillings
Margaret Hobbs
Ann Hodges
Mickey Holton
George Hooper
Susan Hoyle
Kim Hutchens
Rodney Joyce
Peter Kell
Richard Kell
Jo Kimberlin
Phillip Kirk
Patricia Knight
Theresa Lange
Linda Langston
Jerolyn Martin

Grace Maynard
Ashley McArthur
Denise McBreaty
Molly Simon McClellan
Sharon McCrary
Edythe Edwards
    McKinney
Kaki McKnight
Gary Milhollin
Vincent Monzel
Jim Moore
Jim Myers
Diane O'Conner
Lynn Clayton Peterson
Damon Pike
Phyllis Post
Deena Richey

Jerry Roscoe
William Russo
Marilyn Servis
Beth Singleton
Dianne Smith
Margaret Smoot
Martha Spenger
Cecile Zaugg Srodes
Jean Stuckey
Jane Suddreth
Mary Trimble
Brenda Ward
Wendy Weiner
Marianne Williams
Rebecca Moore Williams
Don Wilson

Special thanks to Susan Asmus Cobb for help compiling this list.

a staff reunion

Pictured on these pages are just some of the many, much-appreciated staff members who enabled Jim Broyhill to serve his constituents over decades.

The North Carolina Award

P resented annually since 1964, the North Carolina Award recognizes significant contributions to the state and nation in the fields of fine art, literature, public service, and science. The award was established by the General Assembly in 1961, and though given by the governor, the award is administered by the Department of Natural and Cultural Resources.

In 2015, Senator James T. Broyhill was recognized for his career of public service to North Carolinians. His fellow recipients that year were:
Anthony S. Abbott - Literature; Anthony Atala, MD - Science;
A. Everette James, Jr., MD - Fine Arts; Howard N. Lee - Public Service;
Patricia McBride - Fine Arts

Atala, Abbott, Lee, Gov. Pat McCrory, Broyhill, McBride, James

Senator James T. Broyhill

I n his first opportunity to cast a ballot, Senator James Broyhill was shocked to see how few of the offices were contested by Republicans. It was an era when success in the Democratic primary in North Carolina was tantamount to election. With quiet resolve he determined to change that course and build a healthier two-party political system in North Carolina. For his business acumen, his long career in both houses of the US Congress, his unassailable ethics and integrity, and his capacity for collaboration, James Thomas Broyhill receives the 2015 North Carolina Award for Public Service.

Statesmanship

Broyhill's father, James Edgar Broyhill, served on the Republican National Committee for twenty-eight years and became known as the state's "Mr. Republican." Jim returned to Lenoir after college to work alongside his father in their nationally-known furniture business. He served as President of his Chamber of Commerce and was Jaycee's Outstanding Young Man of the Year before setting his sights on the US House. Charles Jonas, Representative from a neighboring district and the sole member of the GOP in the North Carolina delegation, set the model. The 1962 race, a close one, propelled Broyhill to twelve terms in the House. In 1964, when Lyndon Johnson carried 87 of 100 counties, Broyhill was reelected comfortably.

The Energy and Commerce Committee was Broyhill's home on Capitol Hill for much of his tenure. There he took the lead in passing the Consumer Product Safety and Clean Air Acts, among other significant pieces of legislation. He excelled at constituent service, and, in the course of his lifetime, he met or worked with 11 of the 15 Presidents. In his day, civility was the standard and not the exception, and Broyhill regularly worked across party lines, all the while maintaining a consistently conservative voting record. His years in the US House ended when Governor James G. Martin, his friend and admirer, appointed him to complete a term in the US Senate, created by the death of Senator John East, where he served with distinction.

In following years, he chaired the North Carolina Economic Development Board and led the state Department of Commerce. In doing so, he achieved new heights in industrial and job recruitment. In 1993 and 2000, Broyhill served as honorary co-chair on successful efforts to pass bond legislation to benefit the university and community college systems. In 2001, he received the I. E. Ready Award in recognition of his tireless efforts.

Appalachian State University and Wake Forest University have been the beneficiaries of Senator Broyhill's service. He served as a member and chair of the board of trustees at Appalachian State and a member of the Wake Forest board of trustees and board of visitors for their management school and medical center. He became an honorary alumnus of Appalachian State in 2000 and received an Honorary Doctor of Laws in 2009. Senator Broyhill maintains an intense interest in history, especially about the Battle of Kings Mountain and the Overmountain Victory National Historic Trail, and is a major supporter of the North Carolina Museum of History.

Now in retirement in Winston-Salem, Senator Broyhill and his wife Louise, are the parents of two children and a late son, six grandchildren, and four great-grandchildren.

Advice on Being a Competent Legislator

Get to know your colleagues. Even if you don't agree with your colleagues on various issues, get to know them. Sometimes, you may be able to get their vote on an issue because of this contact.

• Know the issues. Employ competent legislative aides who can help you with your research and your reading but know the subject well enough that you can articulate the issue to your constituents in simple language everyone can understand.

• Keep track of your voting record. Know exactly why you voted on each issue and write it down.

> **"K**now the issues. Keep your word."

• When you differ with your colleagues, do it in a way that you can come back to them tomorrow and ask for their support on a different issue. Don't fall out with colleagues because they voted differently from you.
You may need them tomorrow on a different issue.

• Once you have given your word, keep your word. There is nothing that will undermine a legislator's success more than to be known as one who cannot be counted on after having given your word that you will support or not support a certain issue. On the other hand, be careful when giving your word. Make sure you have touched all the bases before doing so.

• Plan your time and your day so that you get plenty of rest. Do not go out partying with the guys. Go home to your spouse.

• Stay in close touch with your constituents, by mail, telephone, and frequent visits. Go home often to confer with your constituents and try to make sure they know you have been home. You don't necessarily have to be in the papers ballyhooing an issue — just that you have been home and that you are working. Issue a periodic newsletter. State Rep. Bill Current is excellent at this.

• Plan ahead to take some time off to spend with your spouse and family.

What Do I Believe

I was sometimes asked what I, as an elected member of Congress, believe that helps guide my voting on legislative matters brought before Congress.

Here is a short, condensed outline of my basic political views.

- I am a firm believer in the Rule of Law and that the fundamental law that guides us as a nation is our U.S. Constitution.

- I believe that national economic growth can continue only so long as we have stability of the rule of law.

- I believe the first role of government at all levels is to protect its citizens from harm or threats from harm both at home and from abroad.

- As a former businessman, I believe in the free enterprise system and that the economy works much better by encouraging individual incentive to invest or to go into business. The free enterprise system, operating under a fair system of rules to assure fair treatment of all, has given this nation an economic system second to none on earth.

> "I believe in equal rights and equal justice for all."

- I believe we should rely on the private sector for jobs and economic growth rather than increasing government power and expenditures to provide these job opportunities.

- I believe, as Lincoln said, "That the proper function of government is to do for the people only those things that have to be done but cannot be done by the people for themselves."

- I believe that sound economic growth can be generated only by sound money, and all actions by the government must avoid inflationary deficits.

- I believe that inasmuch as I would want the laws of this great nation to deal fairly with me, I believe in equal rights and equal justice for all.

Why the "Great Divide" in the Center Aisle of Congress?

[Written 2015 as an email to Rick Spangler and Mark Thompson.]

I have been asked this question so many times recently, that I thought I would take a few minutes and jot down my thoughts on this question. Here is the answer:

When I was first sworn into the U.S. Congress back 50 years ago (Jan. 3, 1963), I was one of only eleven Republicans elected from the South, the 11 states of the old Confederacy.

In the Congress before this 87th Congress, there were only seven GOP Representatives from Southern States. In the 1962 election, after the redistricting that took place all across the country after the census of 1960, we added four more GOP Representatives from the South. There was only one lone Republican Senator from the South, John Tower of Texas, who had been elected in May 1961 to take the seat once held by Vice President Lyndon Johnson.

At that time, well over 90% of the Democrats from the South were very conservative. We Republicans got along very well with our Democratic colleagues because there were so many who thought as we did. For example, I recall on numerous occasions I would meet with the Democrats from our state to talk about upcoming issues/votes. We felt comfortable talking with each other even if we did not finally vote the same way.

Then three things occurred that started changing things.

> 1. The "One Man, One Vote" decision of the Supreme Court: (Baker v. Carr) Baker was from Memphis, and said that his Congressional District had not been changed since 1931, and now contained a population that was several times that of more rural Districts in Tennessee, and the districts should be set up so that they had a more equal population. This decision caused redistricting all across the country in the middle of the decade, the first time this had occurred. For example, in North Carolina redistricting occurred twice within the decade, for the 1966 and the 1968 elections. These actions tended to create more Republican-leaning Districts across the South.

2. Passage in 1965 of the Voting Rights Act.

The Voting Rights Act requires that all Congressional redistricting plans treat minorities fairly. In addition, the plans are subject to review by the Justice Department. The result has been that in all the Southern states, Congressional District lines are drawn so as to actually favor the election of minorities. (For example, the N.C. 12th which extends up I-85 from Charlotte to Greensboro.) When this type of redistricting occurs, it tends to create more conservative, Republican voting districts in the suburbs.

3. Beginning after World War II. we have witnessed "white flight" from inner cities to the suburbs. All across the country, as redistricting takes place, this has created Republican-leaning districts and solid Democratic-voting districts.

With these three factors impacting the creation of Congressional Districts, the districts have become more Republican or more Democratic in their voting patterns, as State Legislatures tend to "protect their own," as they redraw Congressional District lines thus making Republican districts stronger by throwing more Republicans in together.

> **"The Congressman who is elected today does not have to talk with the other side."**

The real or decisive voting is done in Primaries; and, in Primaries the fringes tend to be more dominant, not the moderate or the middle. (e.g., remember what occurred in the 2012 election in Indiana and Missouri). For a Congressman to keep his seat, he must satisfy that fringe right or fringe left voter. Thus, the moderate Representatives are few in both parties, and when they do vote with the other side, are usually punished for doing so. The Congressman who is elected today does not have to talk with the other side. He has a safe district and as long as he votes to satisfy the fringe right or left in his Congressional District, he can stay there as long as he or she wants.

There are now 97 Republican Representatives from the eleven former Confederate States (vs. 40 Dems). From those same eleven states, there are 16 Republican Senators versus only six Democratic Senators! (In the three border states of Missouri, Oklahoma, and Kentucky, there are 15 GOP Reps, vs. three Dems, and five GOP Senators vs. one Dem.) So, you can easily see that the Republican Party has supplanted the Democratic Party in the South, and the Southern Democratic Representative or Senator is no longer a stalwart Conservative. Consequently, the middle aisle grows wider and wider with fewer and fewer bridges across it.

Political Opponents

1962	Primary: Les Burdick of China Grove, Rowan County
	General Election: Hugh Alexander of Cabarrus County
1964	Bob Davis of Rowan County
1966	Bob Bingham of Watauga County
1968	Basil Whitener of Gaston County
1970	Basil Whitener of Gaston County
1972	Paul Beck of Caldwell County
1974	Jack Rhyne of Gaston County
1976	John Hunt of Cleveland County
1978	No opponent
1980	Lt. Col. Isenhour of Catawba County
1982	No Democratic opponent; Libertarian. Rankin
1984	No opponent
1986	Primary: David Funderburke
	General Election: Terry Sanford

Boards, Commissions, and Awards

Board of Trustees, Appalachian State University (one term as Chairman)
Board of Directors, Appalachian State University Foundation
Inducted as an Honorary Alumnus of Appalachian State University
Board of Directors, Second Harvest Food Bank of North Carolina
Board of Trustees, Wake Forest University (Now Trustee Emeritus)
Board of Visitors, Wake Forest University Baptist Medical Center
Board of Visitors, Babcock School of Management, Wake Forest University
Honorary Co-Chair, Campaign (1993) for passage of statewide bond issues to benefit University System, Community Colleges, State Parks, and Municipal Water/Sewer Projects
Member, Commission to study needs of University and Community College System (2000)
Honorary Doctorate of Laws: Catawba College, 1966
Honorary Doctorate of Laws: Appalachian State University, 2008

James T. Broyhill received the
Charles Raper Jonas Award
for Lifetime Service
to the North Carolina GOP

Honorary Graduate: Richmond Community College, 1994

Honorary Co-Chair, (2000) Campaign for passage of statewide bond issues
to benefit University and Community College Systems.

Received the I.E. Ready Award, the highest award by the North Carolina Board
of Community Colleges

Received The North Carolina Award for Public Service, the state's highest
civilian honor (2015), presented by Governor McCrory

Board of Directors, Senior Services Foundation of Winston-Salem

Board of Directors, North Carolina Museum of History Foundation, Raleigh,
N.C.

Member, U.S. House of Representatives: Jan. 3, 1963 to July 8, 1986

Member, U.S. Senate: July 8, 1986 to Nov. 7, 1986

North Carolina Work First Business Council

Prior to 1962

President, Lenoir Chamber of Commerce (two terms)

Member, Original Planning and Zoning Commission, City of Lenoir

Member, City of Lenoir, Recreation Commission

Chairman, Caldwell County Red Cross Blood Drive: 1956-1957

Named Young Man of the Year by Lenoir Jaycees (1957)

Executive, Broyhill Furniture Industries 1948-1962

One final story that involves Gerald Ford dates back to 1983. My granddaughter, Elizabeth Broyhill, was a 4-year-old, enrolled in the pre-school program at Knollwood Baptist Church in Winston-Salem. It was President's Day and Mrs. Glenda Correll was teaching the little tykes about the U.S. Presidents and why we had a day called "President's Day." A little girl in the class raised her hand and said, "Mrs. Correll, my granddaddy was President!" That little girl's name is Sarah Ford.

Mrs. Correll replied: "Yes, Sarah, and we are so proud of your grandfather, and what he did for our country at a very difficult time in our history by restoring integrity to the office of President." At that, my granddaughter, Elizabeth Broyhill, raised her hand and said, "Mrs. Correll, my grandfather is the President."

Mrs. Correll was very gentle with Elizabeth. She replied, "Elizabeth, we are proud of your grandfather, too. However, you know that Ronald Reagan is our country's President." Elizabeth didn't back down for one minute. She replied, "Yes, but Ronald Reagan works for my Granddaddy!"

- (Excerpted and repeated here from "Presidents I Have Known")

Friendship

The ROMEOs

On coming to Winston-Salem, I became associated with a fine group of men who had lunch together every Monday at the Cloverdale Kitchen in the Cloverdale Shopping Center. We'd gather at a table in the back of the restaurant. We named our group of 10 to 15 men "The ROMEO Club." This stood for "Retired Old Men Eating Out." Two Romeos, Jack Roemer and Bill McCall, still join me occasionally for meals.

The ROMEOs

Below is an invitation to one of our "meetings" in the form of a poem I wrote:

(Romeo: Retired Old Men Eating Out)

You know that it's Monday
When the men go out to lunch.
They're members of the Romeo Group,
And they are a most gregarious bunch.
When we get together, we will have a ball.
The problems of the nation will be solved is my hunch.
So here is a poetic reminder:
Mark on your calendar that you plan to attend.
We will meet at Cloverdale Kitchen at the usual time.
Now my poem's coming to an end.

So, gentlemen, I will see you there.

Jim with Charles Dobbin,
a lifelong friend from Lenoir

Jim with Jack Roemer

Jim with Dr. Bill McCall

Jim Broyill enjoyed and admired this poem. He used it often in sharing his feelings about friendship. Grandchildren read this as part of Jim Broyhill's funeral service.

The Train of Life

a poem by Jim Meador

At birth, we boarded the train of life and met our parents, and we believed that they would always travel by our side. However, at some station, our parents would step down from the train, leaving us on life's journey alone.

As time goes by, some significant people will board the train: siblings, other children, friends, and even the love of our life.

Many will step down and leave a permanent vacuum. Others will go so unnoticed that we won't realize that they vacated their seats! This train ride has been a mixture of joy, sorrow, fantasy, expectations, hellos, goodbyes, and farewells.

A successful journey consists of having a good relationship with all passengers, requiring that we give the best of ourselves.
The mystery that prevails is that we do not know at which station we ourselves will step down. Thus, we must try to travel along the track of life in the best possible way — loving, forgiving, giving, and sharing.

When the time comes for us to step down and leave our seat empty — we should leave behind beautiful memories for those who continue to travel on the train of life.

Let's remember to thank our Creator for giving us life to participate in this journey.

I close by thanking you for being one of the passengers on my train!

A round of golf with (l to r) Tates Locke, Sam Snead, Jim Broyhill, and Gerald Ford

Jim Broyhill and Gerald Ford served together in Congress and remained close friends and colleagues during Ford's Presidency, shown here aboard Air Force One.

Recollections about
Some Legislative Accomplishments

Overmountain Victory National Historic Trail
by James T. Broyhill

My role in establishing the Overmountain Victory National Historic Trail is one of the legislative accomplishments of which I am most proud. Below is a speech I made in 2008.

I read recently where a historian wrote that "the winning of the War for Independence by those early patriots of 225 years ago, changed the course of Western civilization." I believe that, and I believe most historians of today would agree with that statement.

Another great man once said — and I paraphrase — "Every generation should learn and take lessons from history, or they may have to repeat that history."

I am concerned that in our generation we are not familiar enough with the early history of our country, and the tremendous struggle and sacrifices that were made to win for us the freedoms that we enjoy today.

For example, few people know this: Many of the battles that took place during the War for Independence occurred in the South and the final victory at Yorktown was as a direct result of this valiant effort put forth by these early Patriots in the South.

Legislative Accomplishments

The Overmountain Victory NH Trail is a 330-mile commemorative corridor mostly in North Carolina with stretches in NE Tennessee, SW Virginia, and Upstate South Carolina.

The people in this room are the "keepers" of that history, and to you we owe a great debt of gratitude and continued support. So, I am very pleased that your group has been formed for the purpose of "Rediscovering the Spirit of the American Revolution."

Let me tell you the story of how became involved in a part of this story. I can tell you the story of what happened when a small group of men and women became interested in preserving, not only the story of what happened at the Battle of Kings Mountain, but also in identifying and preserving the Trail that those early settlers used to march to the battlefield.

This story begins in the early 1970s. The Battle of Kings Mountain had been commemorated over the years, and the site of the Battle had been made into a National Military Park a generation before, and deservedly so. Back in the 1970s, a group of ordinary citizens, without any state, local, or federal government support, set out not only to commemorate another anniversary of the Battle, but more than that, to identify and preserve the various trails that those early Patriots used as they marched out of the mountains for the purpose of finding the man who was threatening their homes and communities.

There were many men and women who took part in this effort; I am going to mention only four of them. The idea of a commemorative march came up in a conversation between Borden Mace, who was Executive Director of the Appalachian Consortium and Robert L. "Rip" Collins, who operated an outdoor outfitting shop near Boone. Another key figure in the first march was a man by the name of Harry J. Smith, who had been a student at Lenoir High School with me. There were people involved in this project from all parts of the Trail, from east Tennessee, Virginia, western North Carolina and South Carolina. The first march, organized by Borden Mace, Rip Collins, and Harry Smith, took place in 1975, five years before the 200th anniversary in 1980.

Commemorative marches continued from that day forward, culminating in a grand march in 1980, the 200th anniversary of the Battle itself. Along the way, many men, women, and children participated. A number of distinguished public servants took part in various ways. For example, I had an agreement from then Vice President Gerald R. Ford to participate in 1975, but by the time he was to participate, he was President of the United States, and had to cancel his planned visit. He did send his Vice President, Nelson Rockefeller, who was the Grand Marshal of a huge parade that occurred on the streets of Kings Mountain, N.C. On one occasion, General William Westmoreland walked the last day with the

marchers. Over those years, we had Governors of both North Carolina and South Carolina, the Secretary of the Interior, other dignitaries from Raleigh and Washington, Congressmen, and Senators to participate. For example, on one occasion, Senator Sam Ervin took the final steps with the Marchers from the bottom of Kings Mountain to the top.

For that five-year period, the organizers and volunteers who had become the central part of the annual reenactment marches had been working to get the trail itself identified, marked, recognized, and preserved. A few short years before this time, Congress had established the National Historic and Scenic Trails Act, for the purpose of preserving a number

Rep. Jim Broyhill in 1977 with Bill Stronach of Lenoir after the third commemorative march of the Overmountain Victory Trail.

of Scenic and Historic Trails in America. The Appalachian Trail, for example, was a part of the Scenic Trail system. The Oregon Trail and the Lewis and Clark Trail were a part of the new Historic Trails system. The procedure for getting a trail added was quite involved. You had to go through the legislative process twice: first you had to pass legislation for the purpose to establish a study commission to make a study of the proposed trail to determine if it met the criteria, and then, if a favorable report came from the Commission, you had to again introduce legislation to get the trail added to the System. So, I believe it was 1977, I started the legislative process. I introduced a bill to create a study commission. This passed in 1978, and the Commission which was formed took over a year to complete its work. We were most fortunate that we got back a most favorable report; however, time was running out. We wanted this done by the 200th anniversary in October of 1980. The Commission report came out in late 1979, and in early 1980, I introduced legislation to add the Overmountain Victory Trail to the Historic Trails system. This bill was approved in Committee and added to an omnibus bill, which passed in late July of 1980 and was signed by President Jimmy Carter in August of 1980.

There were a number of reasons that the bill passed. One, of course, was because of the determination of literally hundreds and hundreds of people who by now were taking part in the commemorative marches in one way or another. One of the key reasons we were able to get the bill passed was because of Gary Everhart, who you knew as Superintendent of the Blue Ridge Parkway. Many of you don't remember, but Gary was the Director of the Park Service back in the days of the Ford Administration. After the Carter Administration took over in Washington, Gary came back to North Carolina as Superintendent of the Blue Ridge Parkway. He was of immense help and influence in getting not only the study done and completed with a positive report, but in recommending to the House Committee on the Interior that the bill pass. It also didn't hurt that I was on good terms with the Chairman of the full Committee, Morris Udall of Arizona, and also a friend of the Chairman of the Sub-Committee, Philip Burton of California.

One part of this story has only recently been told. Three of the "principal" people in this effort were all students at the old Lenoir High School: Harry J. Smith, Gary Everhart, and me!

(l to r) Author Randell Jones with Harry J. Smith, Senator Jim Broyhill, and Gary Everhart in 2005 at the old Lenoir High School where the latter three were class-mates together, each playing a later role in bringing about the OVNHT.

The story of the battle of Kings Mountain is not complete without also telling the story of the Trail itself. The story of the Overmountain Victory Trail has always been an amazing story to me. Just think of the enormous challenge of mustering men from so many different areas to travel as far as they did, and then have such a significant victory! For example, the militia leaders sent out couriers throughout the area to alert militia leaders to the danger and to urge them to rendezvous at Quaker Meadows near present-day Morganton. One of my wife's ancestors, James Blair, was one of these couriers and is mentioned in the book written by Lyman Draper on the Battle. So, in my judgment, the Trail itself is a significant part of the story.

Today, the Overmountain Victory Trail Association is still alive and well. As you may know, the Park Service dedicates one Ranger for service with the Trail. Paul Carson is filling that role today. However, the real secret to the continued interest in the Trail is that through the years, we have depended on local or private partnerships. In fact, this is one of the reasons it came into existence in the first place, and in my judgment, the Trail is better known today than it was when it was created 25 years ago. The reason is because of these local partnerships. These partnerships consist of not only the OVT Association but other groups as well. The Travel and Tourism Boards of each of the counties through which the Trail runs are partners.

Because of the work of the Park Service in identifying the route of the Trail, local landowners are partners. The Land Conservancy Group is a key partner, having worked with the Park Service to get local landowners to dedicate permanently the portion of the Trail that runs across their lands as a permanent set-a-side, and free forever from development.

In 2010, Senator Jim Broyhill shares some family history that falls along the trail with Paul Carson, the first full-time Superintendent of the Overmountain Victory National Historic Trail.

I am sure that each one of your groups has partners, but perhaps this is one idea or challenge we can take from a meeting like this and that is to work to foster greater partnerships in the communities in which we are located.

Another project that the Association and the Park Service are implementing is a series of educational programs that have been scripted, or written with a great degree of specificity, that can be used in any school in the area. I do believe that educational programs in the schools telling the story of the Carolinas Revolutionary War Trail and the significant part these battles had in winning for us our freedoms, will, in the long run, build the public interest we need if we are to survive and grow. I am not an expert in this area. However, the expert who has had much experience in this area is here today, Mr. Randell Jones, who wrote the OVT Educational program offered to teachers on the NPS Website. I would suggest that you listen to what he has to say on this subject later in the day during some of your sessions. He has had a world of experience in this area.

The Travel and Tourism Industry in both our states is thriving these days, notwithstanding the increased price of gasoline. In North Carolina alone, the travel industry generated over $13 billion of revenues in 2004. I am told that figure represents a 5 percent growth rate over the previous year and accounted for almost 5 percent of this state's jobs. At a time that our manufacturing base is shrinking, I'm thankful that we do have that base of jobs here to help sustain the economy.

Back in the 1960s and 1970s, we did not have such things as heritage tours. I took my family to visit museums, historic sites, and battlefields. We still visit these sites. Just a few weeks ago, I took my wife, daughter Marilyn, and granddaughter Lindsay Beach to visit the Kings Mountain and the Cowpens Battlefields. My granddaughter is a college student and was in the process of writing a paper on the significance of these two battles in bringing an end to the Revolutionary War. While at Kings Mountain, I threw another rock on Ferguson's grave. About two weeks ago, I visited Moore's Creek Battlefield, near Burgaw, and visited the Indian Mounds located near Mount Gilead. These two sites are way off the beaten path, and we did not see many tourists there. But I do believe there is a trend developing, in that more and more people are interested in seeing historical sites. This looks well for the travel and tourism industry because the heritage tourist often stays around longer.

Obviously, a key to promoting our historical sites is a close working relationship with our various Travel and Tourism boards. I am glad to see these forming today and I am especially glad to see that local communities are willing to put some money into these programs. We still don't have enough money in order to properly advertise what we have to offer, but we are much better off than just a few short years ago, when there was zero spending on Travel and Tourism. So, as the economy improves and we solve the budget crisis we are in here in North Carolina, we need to concentrate our efforts on courting our elected Representatives, to tell them our story and to show them what we have accomplished with the bare bones budgets we have had.

One idea I have had that needs some discussions and planning by your group, and that is to provide films of historic heritage tours at our Welcome Centers. We have literally millions of visitors to these centers every year. The centers are

Senator Jim Broyhill tells the story of the Battle of Kings Mountain from a park stage in Elkin during a 2004 commemorative ceremony honoring the battle veterans whose names appear on the roster displayed on the wall.

well staffed, offer a variety of brochures on tourist attractions and also help in making reservations at the travel destinations. This is well and good. However, many travelers don't have an itinerary. They don't know a lot about our two states. I have noticed that when a visitor comes to one of your facilities, one of the first questions they ask is: "Do you have a film?" What if we could put together a short Power Point-type film at each of our centers that highlights the historical significance of sites in that area, as well as the rest of the state? I think it would pay dividends in the future. After all, we don't have to spend money to get these people to come to North Carolina or South Carolina — they are already here. Let's get them to stay awhile so that we can offer them some good old Southern hospitality.

Stephen Ambrose, the late historian, wrote in his last book that the teaching of history is like telling a series of interesting stories. There are so many interesting stories that can be told about the Carolinas Revolutionary War Trail. Let me conclude by telling you a few short stories about some of the men who were the Patriot Leaders of that time:

— John Sevier was six times elected Governor of Tennessee — one time from the "State of Franklin" and five times from the new state of Tennessee. He was elected four times to the United States Congress — one time from North Carolina and three times from Tennessee. The city of Sevierville, Tennessee, was named in his honor.

A statue of John Sevier is in Statuary Hall in the U.S. Capitol Building in Washington, D.C.

— Isaac Shelby was elected as the first Governor of Kentucky and three cities have been named in his honor: Shelby, N.C., Shelbyville, Tenn., and Shelbyville, Indiana.

Senator Broyhill greets and thanks the Sons of the American Revolution Color Guard before he speaks at a ceremony

— Benjamin Cleveland went on to become a local judge. Cleveland County in North Carolina and Cleveland, Tenn., were named in his honor.

— Joseph McDowell, who fought in both battles — Kings Mountain and Cowpens — served several terms in the North Carolina Legislature and was elected twice to the U.S. Congress. McDowell County was named in his honor.

— Andrew Pickens became an early leader in the state legislature of South Carolina and served one term in the U.S. Congress. Pickens, S.C., was named in his honor.

— William Lenoir went on to become General of Militia forces in the western part of the state, served in the State Legislature, and served as the first Chairman of the Board of Trustees of the University of North Carolina. The city of Lenoir and Lenoir County in North Carolina were named in his honor.

— General Nathanael Greene settled in Georgia and died shortly after the end of the war, but towns, cities, and counties all over the South are named in his honor, including our neighboring city of Greensboro.

— Jesse Franklin was a 20-year-old Lieutenant at the Battle of Kings Mountain. He rose to the rank of Major by war's end. He served in the N.C. House of Commons, the U.S. House of Representatives, and the U.S. Senate where he served as President pro tempore. He was elected Governor of North Carolina in 1821 for one term and we are told he would have been elected for more terms

Senator Broyhill is pleased to cut the ribbon for a newly installed interpretative wayside exhibit along the Overmountain Victory National Historic Trail, this one in Elkin in September 2010.

if he had not met an untimely death in 1823. He is buried in the Guilford Courthouse Battlefield Park.

— Daniel Morgan served as a commander under Nathanael Greene and after the war went back to his home in Virginia. The City of Morganton is named in his honor.

— Joseph Winston returned to Surry County, where he was elected five times to the N.C. Senate, twice as a presidential Elector, three times to the United States Congress, and served as a Trustee of the University of North Carolina. He is buried at Guilford Courthouse Battleground. The town of Winston, which later became the city of Winston-Salem, was named in his honor.

What happened to the British Commanders?

— Lt. Col. Banastre Tarleton saw continued action up until Yorktown. After the war, he returned to England, became a General and also became a member of Parliament, and lived to the ripe old age of 80. Later in life he wrote his memoirs, which you can read in the local library, but in his memoirs, there is no admission that his defeat at the Battle of Cowpens led to the final British defeat.

— Major General Lord Cornwallis — Although his surrender at Yorktown decided the war in favor of the Americans, Cornwallis remained in high esteem at home. In 1786, he was appointed as the Governor General of India. In that post, he brought about a series of legal and administrative reforms that were set in regulations known as the Cornwallis Code. He was appointed Viceroy of Ireland in 1798 and served in that capacity for three years. In 1805 he was reappointed as Governor General of India but died in India some two months after his arrival.

In October 2012, Senator Broyhill thanked those in the North Wilkesboro audience who, as members of the Overmountain Victory Trail Association, have continued to reenact annually since 1975 the march which gave birth to the OVNHT, helping "keep the story alive."

— Major Patrick Ferguson — The Major, who was commander of the British Force camped on the top of Kings Mountain, was killed at the Battle of Kings Mountain, before notification reached him of his promotion to Lt. Colonel. He still lies on the mountainside of Kings Mountain. His grave site is easy to find and to see. A plaque has been erected there in memory of Lt. Col. Patrick Ferguson. The story is told that there were two women in the Ferguson Camp on top of Kings Mountain. Their names were Virginia Paul and Virginia Sal. We are told that they were listed on the regimental roles as "Laundresses." However, we are also told that they spent the night in Major Ferguson's tent, so we have some reason to believe that doing the laundry was not their total duty. As the battle progressed, Virginia Paul made her escape down the hill, and we are told that she stopped long enough to tell the Patriot leaders that Ferguson could be identified by the red checkered shirt that he was wearing. Virginia Sal, however, was struck by a stray bullet and killed. She along with Major Ferguson were buried in the same gravesite. So, Ferguson's remains lie there, under a huge pile of rocks about ten feet high. Ferguson was so hated in the west that for decades the people of that area, when they passed Ferguson's grave, would throw a rock onto it. I was there recently and threw one

In December 2008, Senator Broyhill was pleased to see the first OVNHT display installed along the trail, this one part of an exhibit in the Wilkes Heritage Museum in Wilkesboro.

more rock on Ferguson's grave.

There are so many fascinating and interesting stories we could tell our visitors. Our challenge is to use what resources we have, band together with support groups in each of your communities and put out the welcome mat. If we build it, they will come!

Earlier, I told you a little about the early leadership of two men in the effort to get recognition of the Trail. These two men were: Robert L. "Rip" Collins, of Boone, and Harry J. Smith, formerly of Lenoir, and now a resident of Laurel Bloomery in Tennessee.

In 1980, as these two men were riding to a meeting of the Overmountain Trail Association, Rip turned to Harry and said: "Harry, I don't know if we will ever accomplish anything else in our lives, but what we have accomplished here is important."

Yes, indeed. What they and the many others did in the 1970s to revive interest in the Battle of Kings Mountain was important. But it continues to be important that we keep the memory of these great events and accomplishments alive for future generations. That is our task, pure and simple. It is not an easy task, but the rewards are great; and that is, a future generation that knows something of its past, with a greater appreciation of the sacrifices of past generations, and a clear picture of what they need to do to pass on a better world to their children and grandchildren.

The results of the victory — Conclusion

The most immediate result of these two victories was in the minds of the people of the South. These two victories sent a wave of hope through the Carolinas and Georgia. It also had the effect of discouraging loyalists from actively joining the British cause. Cornwallis was never able to replace the regulars he lost at Cowpens and Kings Mountain. When he left his base and proceeded on a march through North Carolina, the patriot partisans in South Carolina rose in revolt. And eventually the British had to abandon all the forts they had established and to retreat to the port cities of Charleston and Savannah. Greene's army was still too weak and under-provisioned to fight a pitched battle, so they retreated in face of Cornwallis' advance. However, Cornwallis had to abandon his wagons, his tents, and much equipment. Even all the rum casks were smashed. Although Greene was forced to retreat after the battle of Guilford Courthouse, Cornwallis had lost so many men and the country was so much "up in arms" against him, he retreated to the port city of Wilmington to refit his small army. From there he marched to the Chesapeake, and ended up at Yorktown where he thought the British navy would either reinforce him or take him away to safety. That did not occur, because the French Navy got there first, along with the Continental Army commanded by General George Washington. After the surrender of Cornwallis' army on October 19, the war was won. This occurred only one year after the Battle of Kings Mountain and only nine months after the victory at the Battle of Cowpens, the two battles that signaled the beginning of the end. •

[Images courtesy of Randell Jones]

Consumer Product Safety Act

from Nancy Nord

I t's hard to know how best to describe the significant policy contributions that Senator Broyhill made in so many different areas. Others will describe his accomplishments in shepherding through the legislative process "big" bills such as the landmark Clean Air Act. My exposure to him was on "smaller," but no less important, legislation. There may well not have been a Consumer Product Safety Commission (CPSC) but for the efforts of "Mr. Broyhill" (that is what I always called him). He was a central part of the coalition that was able to find a path through the complicated trade-offs that led to final passage of the Consumer Product Safety Act (CPSA) in 1972. And American consumers are safer because of those efforts. Similarly, he was critical in helping forge the agreements that resulted in the very important Magnuson-Moss Warranties/FTC Improvements Act that set guardrails for consumer product warranties and also codified the Federal Trade Commission's (FTC) rulemaking authorities. I worked on those bills as an attorney representing industry interests. But my most direct and most meaningful experience was working for Mr. Broyhill as Commerce Committee counsel when he was the ranking Republican on the Committee.

During the six years from 1976 to 1981 that I worked for the Committee, Mr. Broyhill was always available and totally engaged in the legislative efforts of the Consumer Subcommittee which I staffed. His engagement was in addition to his having full jurisdiction of the Committee within his focus. During that time, we worked most closely on three issues.

The first issue involved the Federal Trade Commission. During the Carter Administration, the FTC Chairman, Michael Perschuk (a former counsel to the Senate Commerce Committee), implemented quite an activist agenda, proposing rules regulating a wide variety of industries. Mr. Broyhill was concerned that the rules being implemented by the FTC were not based on hard evidence and that the views of those affected had not been adequately considered. Consequently, he proposed legislation to put in place procedural safeguards that the agency must follow when promulgating industry-wide rules. Mr. Broyhill was able to bring along the Democratic Senator from Kentucky, Senator Wendell Ford, as his chief ally in the Senate and that bipartisan effort resulted in passage of significant legislation reforming the regulatory process at the FTC.

The second issue involved amendments to the Consumer Product Safety Act. The CPS Commission, as a young agency, only set up in 1972, was trying to find its way in establishing processes for implementing its mission. Again, under leadership appointed by the Carter Administration, the CSPC initiated processes best described as "regulating by press release." The agency would issue press releases suggesting safety issues with products before it had adequately investigated and marshalled the facts to show the safety hazard. After a series of oversight hearings, Mr. Broyhill, again working with a bipartisan group of Members in both the House and Senate, oversaw the passage of the 1981 amendments to the CPSA, which made important improvements to the operations of the CPS Commission.

The third issue involved oversight and legislation involving the National Highway Traffic Safety Administration (NHTSA). Although we worked on several bills dealing with NHTSA, my most memorable experience was working with him on legislation dealing with the agency's efforts to put in place automatic passive restraints systems, aka, air bags. Under the direction of Administrator Joan Claybrook, NHTSA was adamant that air bags be mandatory on all US automobiles on a schedule that was impossible for auto makers to meet with the technical reliability required for such systems. Mr. Broyhill worked closely with Commerce Committee Chairman John Dingell and ultimately prevailed on legislation that put in place a more realistic schedule for rolling out this evolving technology.

On a more personal note, I found Mr. Broyhill was always available to offer a word of advice and encouragement when I needed it. When I was a Commissioner and then Acting Chairman of the CPSC, I would, on occasion, reach out to him just to bring him up to date on what the agency was doing. His words of advice were always practical and valued. I am attaching a quick email exchange with him and former Rep. John Y. McCollister that illustrates this. As I note in this email, he taught me to cut through all the "can't be done's" to get to practical solutions. This was an invaluable lesson and one I continue to carry with me. His many legislative accomplishments were a result of his ability to forge alliances and earn the respect and trust of his colleagues on both sides of the aisle and in both chambers. If only more legislators would follow the example he set.

Email exchange with John Y McCollister:

Nancy Nord 7/26/2012
John Y, I learned so much from you and from Senator Broyhill, including cutting through all the "can't be done's" to get to pragmatic solutions.
You would not believe the pace at which this agency is pumping out regulations

and certainly with no cost-benefit analysis. Our chair recently said that was too onerous. If only you two were back here in DC . . . . Nancy

From: John Y McCollister
To: JMcCollister; kbmccollister; pat; mccmission; SMcCollister; brucemcc; John Stokes McCollister; Steve McCollister
Cc: jdforest; jopatcramer; lesashafer; LHanson; tes-msco; dphillip
Sent: Thu, Jul 26, 2012 12:04 pm
Subject: FW: Fischer Campaign Newsletter
This will tell you why I like Jim Broyhill so much. We served on the same Commerce Committee for six years. Great family, too.
I miss him a lot. John Y

From: James T. Broyhill
Sent: Wednesday, July 25, 2012, 3:19 PM
To: 'John Y McCollister'
Subject: RE: Fischer Campaign Newsletter
I was interviewed last week for an hour program before a live audience. I was asked what I would do if I were President to deal with our economic problems. I said that I would:
1. Freeze all Taxes and regulations for five years to give certainty to the business community;
2. After having dealt with the tax question, I would LOCK up all the Congressional leaders in a room and not let them out until they had come up with a meaningful plan to deal with the debt and the deficit;
3. I would issue the necessary Presidential orders to authorize production of all kinds of energy: green, black, or whatever so that within ten years we would again be energy self-sufficient in this country, and
4. Finally, I would order an immediate full inquiry and study of all our trade agreements with every trading partner we have for the purpose of opening up markets to U.S.-made goods.
I got a standing ovation from the audience.
Senator Jim Broyhill

> **Nancy Nord** is a former Chairman of the Consumer Product Safety Commission and Director of Federal Government Relations for the Eastman Kodak Company. Previously, she served as general counsel to the Council on Environmental Quality at the White House, an attorney at the Federal Communications Commission, and Republican Counsel to the U.S. House of Representatives Commerce Committee, specializing in product liability and consumer protection

legislation. She also practiced law at the Washington, D.C., law firm of Verner, Liipfert, Bernhard, McPherson and Hand, and served as the first executive director of the American Corporate Counsel Association.

Amendment to the Selective Service Act

from Cecile Srodes

When the military draft was in effect, there was a "sole surviving son" provision, which meant that the last son in a family which had lost other sons to military service was exempt from the draft. Jim Broyhill spearheaded an effort to change this requirement to provide that, if one son was killed in military service, no additional sons in the family could be drafted. The loss of one son was all that any family should be expected to bear.

The context of this legislation was the increasing controversy about the Vietnam War, the draft, and many anti-war demonstrations in Washington and elsewhere. A bill to end the draft was brought to the House floor and was defeated. (This was the expected result, but having the vote put people on the record as being for or against the draft.) The Broyhill bill to amend the sole-surviving-son provision was considered at the same time. It passed with bipartisan support, although the Broyhill bill was opposed by the Pentagon and the Chairman of the House Armed Services Committee, Edward Hebert. those provisions were subsequently enacted and remain on the books today. The military draft was ended by the Pentagon in (January 1973) and has not been reinstated. It could be argued that passage of this bill to amend the sole-surviving-son provision and the many positive votes on the bill to end the draft led the Pentagon to end the draft sooner than might have happened otherwise.

Broyhill's sponsorship of this legislation arose from the situation of a family in his Congressional district. (This is the story as I remember it, although I may have a few details wrong.) A distraught mother, a widow, contacted the office to request that the Army give her son on active duty serving in Vietnam a hardship discharge so he could help on the farm. She had lost two (or perhaps three) other sons in Vietnam. Because she had one younger son still at home, the Army said her soldier son was not eligible for discharge because he was not the "sole surviving son." While the Broyhill office was working to persuade the Army to discharge this soldier, he was killed in combat. Needless to say, this tragic story made a compelling case for revising the sole-surviving-son provision.

Cecile Srodes (then Cecile Zaugg) began her career on Capitol Hill with a job in the office of Congressman James T. Broyhill in late 1966. She was hired as a caseworker and moved up to become legislative assistant. Upon the death of longtime Administrative Assistant Vince Monzel, the Congressman promoted her to fill that position. She was responsible for overseeing the operations of the Washington office and two district offices, in Lenoir and Gastonia. In 1975, she left Capitol Hill to attend law school full time at the Washington College of Law at American University, graduating cum laude in 1979. She returned to Capitol Hill to work for another Congressman, then joined the staff of the House Energy and Commerce Committee, on which Broyhill was Ranking Republican, in June 1981. In July 1984 she was named Director of Legislative Affairs for the U.S. Securities and Exchange Commission. In late 1987, she joined the Washington office of the New York Stock Exchange, from which she retired in 2005. She continued to keep in contact with Senator Broyhill through the years until his death.

Vice President Gerald Ford

by Cecile Srodes

Not all achievements in Congress were accomplished through legislation. For example, when Vice President Spiro Agnew resigned in October 1973, President Nixon wanted to appoint John Connally, who had served as his Treasury Secretary, as Vice President. (This was the first time the vice-presidential vacancy provision of the 25th Amendment had been implemented. It requires a majority vote of both the House and Senate to confirm.)

Gerald Ford and Jim Broyhill
were close colleagues in Congress.

Republican Members of the House of Representatives were strongly opposed to Connally, a former Democrat who had been Governor of Texas from 1963-1969, and were united in their support for House Minority Leader Gerald Ford. I recall that they met in the Broyhill office late one afternoon and decided to go to the White House that evening to meet with Nixon and to push for Ford's appointment. Ford had bipartisan support in the House; he was nominated, confirmed, and sworn in in the House chamber on December 6, 1973.

I remember my pride and excitement sitting in the House Gallery for the swearing in, and knowing that my boss had been an important part of the process.

Presidents I Have Known

by Senator James T. Broyhill

Senator Broyhill's remarks on Feb. 11, 2010, the week of President's Day, as the after-dinner program presented to the Primetimers gathering at First Presbyterian Church, Winston-Salem.

We are gathered here on the week of President's Day. President's Day is the day we pause and reflect on those men who have led this nation over the past 225 years. It was 225 years ago, in March 1789, that our first President, George Washington, took his oath of Office in New York.

By federal law, President's Day is officially Washington's Birthday. Washington was born on February 22; however, the observance of Washington's Birthday on the third Monday of February, results from the Uniform Monday Holiday Act of 1968 (which became effective in 1971).

Senator James T. Broyhill with Pres. Reagan and V-Pres. Bush

Presidents I Have Known

In the late 1980s, retailers and advertisers began playing a key role in changing the name of the holiday to President's Day. So, in our day, this February holiday has become well-known for being a day on which retailers hold sales. By the way, since 1862, there has been a tradition in the United States Senate that George Washington's Farewell Address be read in the U.S. Senate on his birthday. That will be done on February 22, not today.

In my remarks and the PowerPoint presentation I give today. I am NOT going to talk to you about all of our Presidents. I am going to share with you tonight some facts, some stories, and a number of pictures of the last 15 Presidents; that is, those men who have been President since I have been alive. I have met or known 11 of these men and will share with you some of the pictures made with them that I saved over the years and give you some history of each President's administration, plus some stories about them you may not have heard before.

Calvin Coolidge

I have been around for a while. Longer than most people in this room. When I was born, Calvin Coolidge was President. Although he did not leave a long record of achievement while in the White House, he was very popular during his day and age. A lot of children born in that day were named for him. For example, my cousin, Calvin Howell, was named for him. Calvin Coolidge, born

President Calvin Coolidge

in Vermont, educated in Massachusetts, and former Governor of Massachusetts, was President during a period of economic prosperity. He was placed on the ticket with Warren Harding in the election of 1920 because of the nationwide publicity he received in 1919, as Governor of Massachusetts when he broke the City of Boston Police officers strike by sending in the National Guard. The statement he made at the time was widely publicized across the Nation: "There is no right to strike against the public safety by anyone, anywhere, anytime." It made him a national hero.

He learned that he was the President (on the death of President Warren Harding) while visiting Vermont. By the light of a kerosene lamp, he took the oath of office from his father who was a Notary Public, while holding his hand on the Coolidge family Bible.

In 1924, he was elected to a full term in the White House, yet, as written by Walter Lippmann; "He had a talent of effectively doing nothing!" Yet he loved to be pictured with people like Baseball players, Boy Scouts, and Indians.

Calvin Coolidge was a man of very few words. "Silent Cal," he was called.

His wife, Grace Coolidge, recounted a story about his inclination to say little. One Sunday, he went to church alone. On returning home, his wife asked him: "What did the Preacher talk about this morning?" "Sin," Coolidge replied. "Well, what did he say about it?" asked Grace. "He's against it!" replied Silent Cal.

Another story his wife told is that Dorothy Parker, the newspaper columnist, sitting next to Coolidge at a dinner party. She confided to him that she had bet she could get more than two words of conversation from him. Without so much as looking up, he quietly replied: "You lose."

His last will and testament consisted of only 23 words. "Not unmindful of my son, John, I leave all my estate, both real and personal, to my wife, Grace Coolidge, in fee simple."

If word of how you can write a short will like this gets around town, I am afraid a number of our prominent attorneys may go out of business.

On learning of his death in 1933, the columnist Dorothy Parker posed the question: "How could they tell he was dead?"

Herbert Hoover

Herbert Hoover was one of the most maligned Presidents of all our Presidents. He was a successful mining engineer, had spearheaded the relief for war-torn Europe, and served as Secretary of Commerce in the Harding/Coolidge Administration. In 1928, he was elected President by a landslide, and four years later was one of the most hated men in America. He became President during a

(l to r) President Herbert Hoover (seated), Joe Kennedy, Bernard Gimbel
James E. Broyhill, Gen. Robert Wood (seated)

period of economic prosperity, and just a few months into his Administration, the country was suddenly in the depths of a Depression that lasted for years. History shows that his Administration tried to take drastic steps to stem the tide during the early days of the Depression, but they came too little, too late or were the wrong economic medicine to get the economy rolling again. For example, Hoover asked Congress to raise taxes, and to raise tariffs on imports and world trade plummeted. Instead of protecting American jobs, the Smoot-Hawley tariff bill is widely blamed for setting off a worldwide trade war which only made the country's and the world's economic ills worse. Ironically, the public works programs he had requested from Congress were later enacted into law under the leadership of Franklin Delano Roosevelt.

I met Herbert Hoover on two occasions. My late father was a friend of Herbert Hoover. In 1949, during the early days of our courtship, my father took my wife, Louise, and me to meet Herbert Hoover in his Waldorf Apartment in New York City. On that occasion, my father presented President Hoover with a gift: a jar of Wilkes County sourwood honey! He had had this before and dearly loved it.

I never had my picture taken with Herbert Hoover; however, here is a photo taken with my late father, J.E. Broyhill. I was present when this picture was taken.

Included in the picture are President Hoover, General Robert Wood, President of Sears Roebuck, Joe Kennedy, the father of President Kennedy, and the owner of the Merchandise Mart in Chicago, Bernard Gimbel, the President of Gimbel's Department Stores, and my father, J.E. Broyhill, founder of Broyhill Furniture Industries.

In later years, Herbert Hoover's reputation, and especially his reputation for public service, was enhanced by his appointment by both President Truman and President Eisenhower, to a blue-ribbon commission to reorganize the executive departments of the federal government. This commission became known as the Hoover Commission.

Franklin Delano Roosevelt

Assuming the Presidency in the depths of the Great Depression, Franklin Roosevelt helped the American people regain faith in themselves. Although he was a polio victim, he was never photographed in a wheelchair or using a cane.

President
Franklin Delano Roosevelt

His fireside chats and radio addresses to the people brought hope as he promised vigorous action to stem the Great Depression that was playing havoc with the American economy. It was always ironic to me that the man who was the architect of the modern Democratic Party, the father of the New Deal, the man credited with reviving the American economy from the Great Depression, and saving the free world in World War II, and a man who served as President longer than any other American, elected an unprecedented four times, had so few monuments erected in his honor and memory in the nation's capital.

Harry S. Truman

Assuming the Presidency on the death of Franklin Roosevelt, Truman felt unprepared, and the country was skeptical as to his ability to handle the job or to get reelected. Truman surprised all his critics and opponents, by not only getting reelected notwithstanding huge impediments, but in taking firm stands on the economy, managing world affairs in the early days of the Cold War, founding of the United Nations, and in managing a war that broke out in Asia. Within days of assuming office, he made the firm decision to use the new atomic weapon against Japan. There are men in this room who will tell you they are alive today because Harry Truman had the guts and fortitude to make this decision.

I have vivid memories of this era because the Truman election year of 1948 was the first year that I cast a ballot. During that year, I had the honor of driving and escorting through the state of North Carolina some of his political opponents that year: Senator Bob Taft, Governor Harold Stassen of Minnesota, and Governor Thomas Dewey of New York.

Harry Truman had little chance of winning election to a full term in his own

right in 1948. Truman had made some "gutsy" calls, but along the way alienated powerful political interests in the country. His proclamation of the Truman Doctrine was widely accepted, that is, the containment of Communism, to try to shore up the fledgling democracies of Europe to withstand the rising tide of Communists.

President Harry S. Truman surprised everyone by winning the 1948 election, even the newspapers already printing their early edition.

This was first applied in Greece and eastern Europe and followed by the adoption of the Marshall Plan (named for then Secretary of State George Marshall), providing economic aid to worn torn Europe. Truman ended segregation in the armed forces, alienating the Dixiecrats. He used the power of the Presidency to break the strikes in the steel industry and the national railroad strike, thus alienating Big Labor.

The Democratic Party was split three ways that year (1948). The Dixiecrats were supporting Strom Thurmond for President, and the Progressive Democrats were supporting Henry Wallace. Thomas Dewey was the Republican candidate. With those odds against Truman, the smart money was on the election of Governor Dewey for President. Truman just went out on his "whistle stop campaign tour," the famous "Give 'em Hell, Harry" campaign tour of the country, and whipped them all.

Dwight D. Eisenhower

Dwight Eisenhower was one of the most popular Presidents of the last century. He graduated from West Point in the Class of 1915. This class is called, "The Class on which the stars fell," because one-third of the members of this class made the rank of Brigadier General or higher. Two members of this class made five-star rank.

He married Mamie Dowd in 1916, shortly after graduating from West Point. His great prestige and popularity as the victorious commanding General of the Allied forces in achieving victory over the Axis forces, propelled him into the White House. The political cry at the time was: "I like Ike!" and the American people liked and kept him in the White House for two terms. This was a time that America was rebounding from World War II, and at a time the Cold War was heating up in some areas of the world.

Representative Broyhill and Louise with former President Dwight Eisenhower

I had the privilege of meeting President Ike on three occasions. The first time, Louise and I were fortunate to have an opportunity to meet with President

Eisenhower at a gathering in Pinehurst in 1962, and to receive his endorsement for election that year.

Few people remember that Ike was a rather good artist. Here are some examples of his work.

John F. Kennedy

John Kennedy was the youngest man to be elected President. He was the youngest to die in office. His Administration lasted for only 1,000 days, yet he is

President John F. Kennedy

still revered and honored as a great President. The fact is that he advocated much but got very little cooperation from Congress in enacting his programs. Ironically, his successor, Lyndon B. Johnson, although he was not a very "lovable" person, got the Congress to enact the Kennedy programs and more. There are great memorials to President Kennedy in Washington, and very few memorials to Lyndon Johnson.

Kennedy's favorite rocking chair was a straight back wooden rocking chair. The chair was made in Asheboro, N.C., by the P & P Chair Co., owned by Mr. W.C. Page. This company is not in business today due to the passing of Mr. Page.

I did have the opportunity to meet President Kennedy on two occasions and had my picture taken with him. Unfortunately, the picture did not survive. I had known his brother-in-law, Sarge Shriver, and my father knew his father, so we had had a nice chat when the picture was taken, and I am still trying to find it.

One of the popular new programs initiated by Kennedy was the Peace Corps. This program was directed by the President's brother-in-law, Sergeant Shriver. Shriver was a frequent visitor to my office. In fact, Sergeant Shriver was a frequent visitor to my office in Lenoir in the 1950s, when I was in the furniture business. Sarge was an executive with the Merchandise Mart in Chicago, owned at that time by his father-in-law, Joe Kennedy, and Sarge was making an effort to get Broyhill Furniture to move our showrooms to the Merchandise Mart.

Lyndon B. Johnson

The Administration of Lyndon Johnson had an incredible legislative record, a close second to the Administration of Franklin Roosevelt. His legislative accomplishments take a couple of pages to list. He won election in his own right in 1964 by a landslide, the largest margin of victory in American History. His Great Society programs are still around, yet his Presidency was marred by the quagmire that he entered on escalating the war in Vietnam. I was called to the White House just about every week in those days. Either I was a "spear carrier," that is, a backdrop to his

Rep. James T. Broyhill with President Lyndon Baines Johnson and Robert F. Kennedy

signing a bill into law, or I and other members of Congress were members of the audience as Johnson was haranguing us about backing the President on his Vietnam policy.

Rep. James T. and Louise Broyhill with President and First Lady Johnson

Lyndon Johnson was a large man and could be an intimidating presence. Stories are told, especially during his days as Majority Leader in the U.S. Senate, when this tall man would literally grab members by the lapels of their coats and shake them as he tried to "bulldoze" them into voting his way.

It is rather ironic that within 18 months of winning a landslide victory for the Presidency, and achieving unprecedented legislative victories that his popularity had plunged to less than a 50 percent approval rating. The Vietnam War was heating up. There were riots in the streets over the war and over Civil Rights.

In the 1966 off-year elections, the Republicans gained almost 50 seats in the U.S. House of Representatives, and as the unrest continued, in early 1968, Johnson announced to the nation that he would not be a candidate for reelection, which he would have been permitted to do, in as much as under the 22nd Amendment to the Constitution that on succeeding to the Presidency, he had served less than two years in his first term of office.

Richard M. Nixon

Richard Nixon was elected President in 1968 at a most turbulent time in U.S. History. There had been riots in the streets over Johnson's Vietnam policies, and over Civil Rights at the death of Martin Luther King earlier that year. In 1960,

Representative Broyhill with
President Richard M. Nixon

Nixon had lost the race for the Presidency to John F. Kennedy. In 1962, he had lost the race for Governor of California, and it was generally thought that his political career was finished. However, in 1968, he made a political resurrection. He won the election of 1968 against significant odds against him.

In the election of 1968, George Wallace of Alabama was heading a third-party effort for the Presidency, and no one thought Nixon had a chance to be elected.

I first met Richard Nixon when he was Vice-President. My father was the Republican National Committee member from North Carolina and had come to know Nixon well. In 1957, while driving through suburban Washington, we saw the Vice President mowing his lawn, and stopped to chat for a while. In 1958, he was a guest at our family home in Blowing Rock. In 1960, I was a member of the greeting committee on his Presidential campaign visit to Greensboro. In 1964, Nixon made two campaign appearances for me, both in Salisbury. At that time, he was not in office and was practicing law in New York. During the Nixon Administration, I was in the White House often. Because of the unrest in and around the nation's capital, Nixon started the practice of having religious services in the White House and invited our family to join him and others on these occasions. I was with him in the Oval Office on more than one occasion.

I will tell you a story of the last time I saw Richard Nixon. After the election of 1989, my friend, Governor Jim Martin, had a small campaign deficit and arranged for a fund raiser here in Winston-Salem for the purpose of helping him pay off his campaign debt. Governor Martin asked Richard Nixon to speak at this occasion. Governor Martin's staff called President Nixon to tell him that Senator Broyhill would meet him at the airport.

Rep. James and Louise Broyhill with President Richard M. Nixon

I was told that Nixon's reply was: "I would rather be met by Senator Broyhill's pretty blond wife!" This terrible picture was taken on that occasion, yet Nixon had the ability to laugh at himself since he signed it: "What a picture! Richard Nixon." [Image shown is not the picture referenced.]

I must confess, that I never saw the "dark" side of Richard Nixon and was most disappointed in his behavior that resulted in his resignation from the Presidency. However we do have fond memories of being with him when we saw the "good side" of Richard Nixon.

Gerald R. Ford

I first met Jerry Ford shortly after I was elected to Congress in 1962. It was in that first Republican Conference that he was elected as the Chairman of the Conference and thus became the number-three leader of the House Republicans. In the next Congress in 1964, he was elected the Minority Leader. As a freshman Congressman, I was honored to be named a member of the Republican House Policy Committee, which met with the Leadership on a weekly basis to formulate Republican policy on pending legislation. Thus, I was with Gerald Ford constantly during those years as the Leadership forged their plans to adopt, change, alter the Legislative agenda of the Democratic majority.

In the mid to late 1960s, I was going through political battles back home due to redistricting, and he was kind enough to make campaign appearances on my behalf. I also played golf with Jerry. He was always

Louise and Rep. Jim Broyhill with President Gerald Ford and First Lady Betty Ford

a better golfer than I was. He was a good athlete. In fact, he not only played several sports but coached several sports while at Yale and also while he was in the Navy at the University of North Carolina.

Jerry Ford was in office as President only 29 months, but a lot was packed into those short months. He had to work with a Congress that had a two-to-one majority of Democrats to Republicans. He tried in every way to reduce spending, vetoing 62 bills in that short time. Much of his personal time was spent in foreign affairs—ending the war in Vietnam, continuing negotiations with Russia on arms limitations, and negotiating an end to tensions in the Middle East. He also had to deal with a lagging economy. Gerald Ford was a decent man.

He was a man of integrity and openness. He was unpretentious and always eager to show that there was nothing "imperial" about his Presidency.

One final story that involves Gerald Ford dates back to 1983. My granddaughter, Elizabeth Broyhill, was a 4-year-old, enrolled in the pre-school program at Knollwood Baptist Church in Winston-Salem. It was President's Day and Mrs. Glenda Correll was teaching the little tykes about the U.S. Presidents and why we had a day called "President's Day."
A little girl in the class raised her hand and said, "Mrs. Correll, my granddaddy was President!" That little girl's name is Sarah Ford.
Mrs. Correll replied: "Yes, Sarah, and we are so proud of your grandfather, and what he did for our country at a very difficult time in our history by restoring integrity to the office of President." At that, my granddaughter, Elizabeth Broyhill, raised her hand and said, "Mrs. Correll, my grandfather *is* the President."

President Reagan with Jim and Louise Broyhill and granddaughter Elizabeth at 8

Mrs. Correll was very gentle with Elizabeth. She replied, "Elizabeth, we are proud of your grandfather, too. However, you know that Ronald Reagan is our country's President." Elizabeth didn't back down for one minute. She replied, "Yes, but Ronald Reagan works for my Granddaddy!"

Jimmy Carter
President Carter never used his full name — James Earl Carter, Jr. — he was always "Jimmy Carter." In fact, at his inauguration, he had to get special dispensation or permission to be sworn with the nickname, "Jimmy."

After serving as Governor of the State of Georgia for four years, Jimmy Carter announced his candidacy for President in 1974, almost two years before the election of 1976. This was unprecedented at the time. Today, of course, it is standard practice. In fact, there are some who start their campaigns just after the last Presidential election.

When he announced his candidacy, Jimmy Carter was completely unknown outside of the state of Georgia, yet he took on the better-known names in the Democratic Party and at the Democratic Convention won the nomination on the first ballot. He went on to defeat an incumbent President, which has not occurred very often in American history.

Here are pictures from those days and visits to the Carter White House. In the picture taken in the Oval Office, I was on the front row, until big John Dingell

Rep. Broyhill attends a Rose Garden ceremony with President Jimmy Carter

stepped in front of me! Just recently, there was a big celebration in the nation's capital celebrating that Dingell had served in Congress for longer than anyone in history -- 53 plus years. [Image referenced is not shown.]

Melanie Broyhill attends a
Rose Garden
ceremony with President
Jimmy Carter

Our son and daughter-in-law, Melanie Broyhill, accompanied us to a party in the Rose Garden one summer. Melanie was thrilled to meet the President, but she was even more thrilled to meet Olivia DeHavilland, the movie star who portrayed Melanie Wilkes in the film, "Gone with the Wind." Melanie says that her mother liked that name and named her Melanie. As Melanie and Louise stood talking to the President, Louise just happened to mention that the President had kissed our daughter, Marilyn, at the White House Christmas party. At that the President leaned over and gave Melanie a great big kiss! Here she is being kissed by a President!

Jimmy Carter did not win a second term chiefly because of record inflation, economic uncertainty, high interest rates, and the Iranian hostage crisis. In foreign affairs, Carter did his own negotiating, and is best known for what we call "The Camp David Accords," which helped bring peace between Egypt and Israel.

Ronald Reagan

I first met Ronald Reagan at the Cow Palace in San Francisco during the 1964 election. I was walking with my family through the huge passageway and saw him approaching, walking by himself. I stopped and introduced myself. At that time, I was a freshman Congressman from North Carolina, and introduced him to my wife and small children.

The next time I saw Ronald Reagan was in 1968. In that year, I had a very difficult race for reelection. The state General Assembly had changed my Congressional District and put my home county in with a sitting, incumbent Congressman from Gastonia, Basil Whitener. I was looking for all the help I could get. By

President Ronald Reagan warmly greets Rep. Broyhill in the White House

this time, Ronald Reagan was a well-known political figure. He had been a popular television host and movie star, and in 1966 he had been elected Governor of California. He was in Gastonia attending a political function for me, and I was able to persuade him to take the time to produce a television ad on my behalf.

I will never forget how easily he did that ad for me. We had a carefully prepared, timed script for him. The camera crew set up equipment in a hotel room.

Presidents I Have Known

As Representative and Senator, Jim Broyhill provided welcomed counsel to President Ronald Reagan

Governor Reagan walked into the room and greeted everyone in a most cordial way. He took the script, went over to a chair, sat there for about five minutes or so, got up, went to the mirror on the wall, straightened his tie, and said: "Let's try a take." He stood before that camera, gave the endorsement exactly in the time we had planned, and did it all in one take! Wow! Was I impressed! When I did these political commercials, it usually took me five or six takes to get one right.

The next time I saw Ronald Reagan was in late November of 1980. At that time Reagan was the President-elect. He was staying at the Blair House across the street from the White House. I was the senior Republican on the Energy and Commerce Committee of the U.S. House of Representatives. Gasoline was still

Louise and Jim Broyhill welcomed President Reagan to North Carolina to campaign for candidates

being sold under a refinery/dealer rationing-and-price-control program that had been started years before in the Nixon Administration. I got an appointment with then President-elect Ronald Reagan. Congressman Clarence "Bud" Brown and I met with him at the Blair House to show him how, with the stroke of a pen, he could end this regulatory nightmare the first day he was in office. I am happy to report that that is exactly what he did on taking office on January 20, 1981, and gasoline prices immediately started falling.

Through the next eight years, I was often

in the White House in the Oval Office often, and on more than one occasion was given the honor of being asked to sit with the President at dinner, breakfast, or outdoor barbecues.

George H.W. Bush

I served with George Bush in Congress. I was elected to the Congress in 1962. He was elected to the House in 1966. I have a political confession to make. Frankly, in the 1980 election, he was my first choice for President! I must tell you that the Reaganites never let me forget this, either. George Bush was the youngest Navy pilot in WWII. He completed 58 missions, was shot down, received three Air Medals, and

Senator Jim Broyhill and Louise
with President George H.W. Bush
and First Lady Barbara Bush

received the Distinguished Flying Cross. (DFC). A number of years ago, he started the practice of parachuting from an airplane on his birthday. I saw President George H.W. Bush last fall, and he told me that he is going to do that again next spring on his 85th birthday. George H.W. Bush came from a family with a tradition of public service, and I think that this family tradition pushed him into public service where he served in so many capacities: Member of Congress, Ambassador to the United Nations, Chairman of the Republican National Committee, Ambassador to China, Director of the Central Intelligence Agency (CIA), Vice President, and President.

Again, I would point out to you in this talk on Presidents that political popularity can fade in a heartbeat. Here is a good example of that. George Bush, Sr. achieved unprecedented popularity after the military victory over Saddam Hussein following his invasion of Kuwait. However, just a few short months later, President Bush was unable to withstand the public discontent at home because of a faltering economy and continued high-deficit spending. Thus, he lost his bid for reelection to Bill Clinton.

William Jefferson Clinton

Bill Clinton was and continues to be a master politician. He is an excellent communicator, a close second behind the Great Communicator himself, Ronald Reagan. He is good looking, has his hair, and he is a master at working a crowd and meeting people one-on-one. He was Phi Beta Kappa at Georgetown University, a Rhodes Scholar, graduate of Yale Law School, Governor of Arkansas, and President of the United States, all before the age of 50.

His presidency was marked by a resurgence of the Republican Party, with the Republicans taking control of the House of Representatives in 1995 for the first time in 40 years.

During his last term in office, his Administration was dominated by questions of his personal indiscretions and becoming only the second President in U.S. History to be impeached by the U.S. House. As we all remember, he was tried by the Senate and found not guilty of the charges brought against him (Feb. 12, 1999). He apologized to the nation for his indiscretions and continued to have unprecedented popular approval ratings for his job as President.

President Bill Clinton

I have met him twice, and even though he was on the other side of the aisle from me, I came away both times after only brief meetings with a firsthand glimpse at how this master politician can make people believe he is their best friend.

The first time I met President Clinton was in Ashe County. The Congress had passed some amendments to the legislation protecting the New River, which was first passed back in the early 1970s, legislation that I took a lead in pushing at that time because I had had the honor of representing this area in Congress in the 1960s. The White House arranged for an outdoor event adjacent to the New River itself to showcase his support for environmental causes. The event was attended by thousands of people. I was given the courtesy of a front seat next to the podium.

There were four people on the podium: then Congressman Richard Burr, Governor Jim Hunt, Vice President Al Gore and President Clinton. During the proceedings, both Governor Hunt and Congressman Burr mentioned my name in their remarks and my connection with the passage of the first legislation protecting the New River. Al Gore, a longtime friend and former colleague, with whom I served on the Energy and Commerce Committee for many years, made some remarks and was followed by the President. After all the speeches were over, the four came down to shake hands and started right there where I was seated. I greeted the Congressman, and Governor Hunt. Al Gore, in his "wooden" way, seemed surprised to see me there, even though both the Governor and the Congressman had referred to me only minutes before. When President Clinton came up to me, he grabbed my hand, threw his other hand on my shoulder, and said, "Senator, I heard you were here. You should have been on the platform with us. I have heard so many nice things about you. We need to sit down and talk sometime."

Wow! Within about 30 seconds he had me believing he was my best friend!

I met Bill Clinton again at an event in Washington, D.C., in December of 2005, celebrating the 50th anniversary of service in the Congress of Congressman John Dingell of Michigan. A number of people were on the program, including the Governor of Michigan, the senior Senator from Michigan, the Speaker of the House, and Bill Clinton. I like to say that I "shared the platform" with President Clinton for that occasion, although my remarks came in a special film that was played immediately following President Clinton's remarks. I was seated just a couple of rows back of Clinton, and was able to get to him fairly quickly after the meeting adjourned to say hello, and again, after a minute or two of chatting, and again, I came away with a firm understanding of how his man can get people to say to themselves after meeting him, Hey, this guy is my best friend.

George W. Bush
As I remarked earlier, the Bush family has a significant history in U.S. politics. George W. Bush's grandfather was a U.S. Senator, his father was President of the U.S., his brother was Governor of the State of Florida, and he himself was elected for two terms as the Governor of Texas before being elected President in the millennium year 2000. His entire Administration has been the story of his

To Jim Broyhill
With Best Wishes,

Senator Broyhill visits with
President George W. Bush

leading the nation in a fight against terrorism after the tragic events of September 11, 2001. President Bush's execution of the War on Terror, especially the events surrounding the Iraq War, have completely dominated his Presidency. The new Department of Homeland Security was created to help deal with the longtime problems of fighting terrorism. However, his approval rating, initially very high, has declined to new lows. With respect to domestic issues, he worked with the Congress to enact tax reductions to rejuvenate the economy, passed legislation to reform the Federal Aid to Education program with what he called: "The No Child Left Behind" program. Also, in his Administration we seen massive changes made in Health Care programs, including help for payment for prescription drugs.

As the saying goes, the jury is still out on the final judgment on the Administration of George W. Bush. The war in Iraq goes on, and that war-torn country is going through chaos. Also, relations with other nations are heating up in the Middle East and in Latin America. Bush's

Senator Broyhill and Louise with
President George W. Bush

Republican Party lost control of both Houses of Congress in mid-term election 2006, and little was accomplished in the last two years of the Bush

Administration. During the final months of his Administration, we have witnessed bank failures, massive infusion of cash into the nation's banking system, falling real estate prices, and a recession. George W. Bush could go down in history as a great patriot who won the battle against a new threat to the Homeland, the threat of terrorism, or he could be remembered as the man who lost the war against terrorism and brought on a depression. I am sure historians will long debate the history of actions he has taken in his Presidency. However, the fact is that he left office with the lowest public approval rating of any President since Herbert Hoover.

Barack Obama

Barack Obama was sworn in on January 20, 2009, as our 44th President. However, he is only the 43rd person to be President. Grover Cleveland, the only man to serve two non-consecutive terms in office is both the 22nd and 24th President, so is counted twice.

President Barack Obama

Barack Obama won a long and hotly contested primary campaign to be named as the Democratic candidate for President, and he went on to win the general election by a wide margin. He carried in with him the first solid Democratic majority in the Congress in 35 years. (Heretofore, Democratic margins were much smaller). Thus, he has the luxury of a Congress that will pass just about anything he asks for. Most of our Presidents in recent years have not had this luxury. Two other Democratic Presidents have had this kind of majority behind them: Roosevelt and Johnson. No Republican President has had a Congress with a Republican majority of this magnitude, and often were having to work with a Congress of the different persuasion.

Barack Obama has been an outstanding campaigner, and as the campaign progressed, he drew massive crowds that have never been seen in the political history of the country.

Conclusion

There you have a short outline of 15 Presidents who have served in that office over the past 88 years. In this country, we have a remarkable system of government that has stood the test of time for the past 222 years. Operating under the U.S. Constitution, we have the three branches of Government: the Executive under a President of the U.S., the Legislative branch with the two houses of Congress, and the Court, with the Supreme Court. The Powers and role of each branch of government are spelled out in the Constitution and these powers have been sharpened over the centuries through various laws and past precedents. Our system is different in many ways from the British or the Canadian system. Under our Constitution, there have been checks and balances built into the system. Over our history of the past 220 years, we have seen periods where the powers of the Congress have dominated, and in other eras, the powers of the President have been dominant.

Only 37 percent of our Presidents have been popular enough to be elected for two or more terms —16 including FDR. As you look at the tenure of our Presidents, you will see that most of our Presidents have left office with far less popularity than when they were elected. History also shows that when the country was doing well, the Presidents were doing well. Or is it just the opposite? When the country is not doing so well, the Presidents don't last long in office.

According to the Constitution, the President's powers are derived from the clause that says, "The President shall take care that the laws be faithfully executed." In the past 50 to 60 years, the Congress has given the President enormous powers. However, the Congress still has what we term as "the power of the purse." The President cannot spend money that has not been appropriated by the Congress. According to political scientists, the power of the Presidency is the "power to persuade, and the power to persuade is the ability to bargain." So, the bottom line is that successful bargaining with Congress is essential to Presidential success.

Louise introduces Elizabeth to President Reagan, 1986

Louise greets First Lady Nancy Reagan

Louise with First Lady Pat Nixon

Louise, Marilyn, and Elizabeth with First Lady Barbara Bush

Epilogue

Little-known Facts about Jim Broyhill
by Marilyn Broyhill Beach,
on the occasion of her father's 90th birthday

His favorite TV shows are *Jeopardy!* and Andy Griffith. He has probably watched each Andy Griffith episode 100 times. He often beats the *Jeopardy!* contestants and could easily win the 90-and-over contest, if such a category existed.

He has a great repertoire of jokes and enjoys telling them.

His favorite restaurants are Cloverdale Kitchen and K&W.

He is musical. He played the flute and was, in his youth, a member of an award-winning marching band at Lenoir High School. He has a beautiful singing voice, and was in his church choir for many years.

He has hidden technical talents. He is a computer whiz and once was an airplane pilot.

He was an athlete. He was a runner, excellent swimmer, tennis player, as well as a golfer who could par the toughest courses.

He can cook delicious pancakes.

He loves ice cream: butter pecan is his favorite, and rainbow sherbet. When Ashley was 9, he picked her up every Tuesday from Summit School and took her to Baskin Robbins. They called it their IC Club meeting.

He once picked up a stranger at a bus stop. One day in 1949, in his junior year at Chapel Hill, he offered a ride to a pretty, blonde coed who was waiting for a bus at a bus stop as he was driving to Hope Valley Club in Durham to play golf. The pretty blonde was Louise Robbins, and the rest is history.

He had a budding reporting career. He wrote a newspaper for his father at the furniture market in Chicago that showed great promise as a writer.

He is a survivor. When he was 9, he was stricken with rheumatic fever, fell into a coma, and was not expected to live. Dr. Caroline McNairy, one of our country's first female doctors, ordered a new drug from New York called penicillin and the entire family got on their knees to pray. The next morning, he awoke, but stayed in bed for a year recuperating.

The worst trouble he ever got into was when he played barber shop with his younger sister Bettie and cut off her beautiful long Shirley Temple curls.

He shook hundreds of thousands of hands during his 24 years in politics, and my mother gave him the nickname of "the Jolly Balloon Man" because of all of the balloons bearing his image that we filled with helium to hand out at county fairs.

He is an historian, and regularly gave PowerPoint presentations on a variety of subjects. Ask him about any date in history and he will tell you the reigning king or queen of England from that time. If you are ever playing *Trivial Pursuit,* you should ask him to be your partner.

He has been the author of many pieces of legislation, but he considers the passage of his bill to create the "Overmountain Victory National Historic Trail" one of the best things he did in Congress. It will be there for generations to come.

Mutual Appreciation Shared

by Randell Jones

In the summer of 2015 and before the Senator received his North Carolina Award for Public Service, he sent a note of greetings, a commemorative plaque, and a heartfelt *thank you* to President Jimmy Carter for his role in helping establish something of unique value and significance 35 years before.

As was mentioned prominently in the Senator's award biography, among his many notable contributions to our state and nation, he introduced legislation in 1977 to create the Overmountain Victory National Historic Trail. After Congress passed that bill, President Carter signed it nto law in September 1980, just in time for the bicentennial of the Battle of Kings Mountain. That was the patriot victory so consequential to turning the tide of the American Revolution during the Southern Campaign.

Senator Broyhill sent a plaque to President Jimmy Carter containing 40th anniversary coins commemorating the first walk of the Overmountain Victory Trail in 1975.

That 330-mile national historic trail, lying mostly in North Carolina and now a unit of the National Park Service, came about through the relentless efforts of volunteers, who reenacted every fall, beginning in 1975, the 200-mile march of patriot militiamen from today's northeast Tennessee across the Appalachian Mountains, through North Carolina, and into South Carolina. These modern citizens reenacted volunteer patriot militiamen of 1780 from now five states pursuing British Major Patrick Ferguson, who had threatened to bring his army over the mountains to "lay waste your country with fire and sword."

Following 40 years of annual reenactment marches during which the story of those patriot heroes and their resolve to defend their homeland was shared with tens of thousands of students in communities all along the trail, the Overmountain Victory Trail Association, Inc. issued a commemorative coin for 2015.

Epilogue

During that 40th anniversary celebration, Senator Broyhill sent to President Carter a letter of appreciation and enclosed a plaque including two OVTA commorative coins. The Senator also included my book, *Before They Were Heroes at King's Mountain* inscribed to President Carter, who also wrote about the American Revolution in the South in his novel *The Hornet's Nest*. Senator Broyhill wrote the forewords for my two books about the battle and the Overmountain Victory National Historic Trail.

President Carter sent back to Senator Broyhill a note of gratitude for his kind remembrance of their joint efforts to help bring to all Americans both knowledge of this history and appreciation of its significance.

This militiaman statuette, now at the Burke County History Museum in Morganton, N.C., at the heart of the trail, was presented in September 2020 to recognize Senator Broyhill's service to this trail and the story of the Battle of Kings Mountain, on the 40th anniversary of the Overmountain Victory Trail becoming a national historic trail. The statuette traveled along the OVNHT day-by-day during the 40th Reenactment march in 2014.

Family Remembrances and Eulogies

Laura Beach Dugan
Spoken at the funeral of her grandfather, James T. Broyhill
February 28, 2023

It is quite intimidating to be tasked with speaking in public in remembrance of one of the best public speakers I have known. Really, it's odd to be the one up here in front of you all when in my mind it should be Papa himself. I can hardly recall a family event where he was not the master of ceremonies or otherwise holding court telling stories or giving a speech.

So, yes, Papa's passing leaves a noticeable absence for us, his grandchildren. And yet we know how lucky we were to have had him in our lives so long. The six of us have spent the last week exchanging among us our memories of Papa in his role as a grandfather. It has been a process both sad and heartwarming. I will do my best to share some of these memories, and Penn will follow with some more.

One thing we unanimously agreed upon: Boy, did he love ice cream.

Elizabeth recalled a time when growing up. She was staying at their home when they were awakened late at night to the exterior security alarm going off. It turned out Papa had sneaked out to find the extra freezer out back and was caught red-handed with the spoon midway to his mouth from the tub of ice cream.

Ashley remembers his picking her up from school once a week and always stopping for a detour on the way home to Baskin-Robbins, but only so long as she promised not to tell Lulu! This was, after all, against his doctor's orders for whatever health-conscious meal plan he was supposed to be following at the time.

Whether it was these illicit ice cream trips or treating me to a gourmet meal of fried chicken and strawberry shortcake at the K&W Cafeteria, Papa would never miss ordering dessert. This will always win you big points with grandchildren or, later on, with great-grandchildren who were particularly fond of the rainbow sherbet at Arbor Acres. He was always the first in line at the ice cream station at Sunday brunch. Penn remembers Papa's claiming that blueberry cobbler was an acceptable side dish. And not long ago, I witnessed him eating pumpkin pie at Arbor Acres thinking it should count as a vegetable serving.

We all remember his delight in taking us on train rides at Tweetsie Railroad over the years and treating us to golf cart rides up at Elk River or in Florida. Lindsay remembers that sometimes he would let one of us drive before quickly exclaiming that he was so scared he had turned white. Then he'd pull down his sock to show off his golfer's tan. In later years he took us on rides in his minivan—he really did love a quality minivan!

Unsurprisingly, as a career politician Papa had a healthy sense of self-confidence, and he did not hold back when letting us kids or others know how to do things the "right way," which was his way of course. He taught me how to make a proper handshake, a useful skill I've no doubt used throughout my life. Arguably less helpful was when he would critique my piano performances growing up, suggesting different improvements he would have made playing the piece—never mind that he did not play the piano himself! Ashley remembers his coming back from playing golf with friends and expressing in frustration, "Well I would have had a better time if they would just play the game right!"

But no matter these helpful and less helpful critiques, when it came to his grandchildren, we always knew he was proud of us. He bragged about us constantly to one another, showing off our accomplishments like one of our new business cards or photos of our children, his great grandchildren. Side note: He was convinced every great grandchild took after him or his family in looks. "He has my father's eyes" was said by Papa I think about at least the majority of our kids. The Broyhill genes are strong!

I'm pretty sure the most proud he ever was of me was my starring role as Annie in a community theater production at age 11. He would introduce me to his friends, well into my 30s, as "Laura—she was Annie, remember!" In all seriousness, during one of our last conversations, he told me how proud he was of the job I was doing as a mother to my children, a compliment that meant the world to me. He adored spending time with his great-grandchildren. What a gift that they were able to know Papa!

I think for all of us, Papa's love of Lulu and their over-seven decades of marriage was a real model for us as we go through our own lives and marriages. Their love story, particularly their early years dating and courting, almost obtained a mythological status, and he loved to tell us the story of how they met. In my mind they were true "couple goals." In my dating years, if I got serious enough with someone, the true test would be taking him to meet Lulu and Papa and seeing if he passed muster with them. My poor husband, a native Philadelphian, remembers visiting them for the first time, and having Papa loudly whisper to Lulu, "What did he just say? I can't understand his Yankee accent!" We still aren't sure whether or not he was joking.

Papa was absolutely devoted to Lulu and though she would say she was worried he was so handsome he would get snatched up by some enterprising widow at Arbor Acres, we knew he only had eyes for Lulu. On their 71st anniversary in June, he emailed the six of us a picture of her with the caption: "There must be an error. Someone who looks as young as this cannot have been married for 71 years!"

Papa had so much love for Lulu, for his children, for his grandchildren, great grandchildren, and so many others. I know we all felt that love for him, too. I hope he is looking down on me now and approves of this speech. I'm sure he would have suggestions for how he would have done it better, of course, and I hope that he is enjoying unlimited ice cream up in Heaven!

––––––––

Penn Broyhill
Spoken at the funeral of his grandfather, James T. Broyhill
February 28, 2023

As Laura mentioned, Papa's devotion to the loves of his life: Louise Broyhill and ice cream, really was the hallmark of the man when it came down to it.

But our understanding of this mountain of a man included a few other trademark characteristics and sweet memories.

Papa was one of four siblings, and boy did he love them. We were lucky to see three of them grow old together, oftentimes as playful as children into their 90s.

It was easy for all of us to see why Papa loved his sister, Allene, one of the kindest women I've ever met—she was like walking sunshine. But he also clearly loved his brother, Paul, who could not have been more his foil if they were characters in a book.

And this also brings me to another characteristic of my grandfather, Jim Broyhill—he was chea…—a deeply frugal man.

We remember laughing at stories of Paul sneaking a BLT onto Papa's country club bill from time to time because he knew Jim checked line by line and would get flustered. But Papa knew how to prank him back—my sister told us about a time when she was at a restaurant with Papa. As they were being seated, they realized that Paul was a few tables over with a group of friends. Now for those who didn't know him, Paul was on the other end of the spectrum when it came to things like wine. He would refuse to drink it unless it was the correct vintage and region for that particular meal, and he was not afraid to spend big on his wine! Soon after Papa sat down, he called over and whispered something to the waitress and began his classic giggle. Finally, my sister asked what was going on. Well, my grandfather had sent a bottle of his favorite wine, which cost about as much as a dinner roll, to Paul to see his reaction with his friends around. As Paul got the wine, he seemed confused and began looking around only to find his little brother waiving and laughing.

Papa was playful, especially with us grandkids. He would try his best to entertain us in nice restaurants. To do that he would make a linen napkin into a bunny rabbit. He would hold the rabbit and tell us that we needed to be quiet so that the rabbit wouldn't wake up. If we began to get loud or fidgety, he would pop the napkin in the air and tell us we had scared the rabbit!

He also showed the grandkids love by sharing his favorite pastime with us: golf. He loved the game of golf and loved, even more, passing it on to his grandchildren. He may have been frugal with his money, but he was, as Laura mentioned, generous with his advice.

My brother James and I discussed how Papa would get excited as our games progressed. James remembers how Papa would call friends over to the driving range to point out how far he could hit the ball!

Even his frugality—which did show up on the golf course—was endearing. Papa was both a clever and industrious man used to rallying people to his causes and a man who hated to spend money on golf balls.

He went so far as to bring me and other grandchildren in on his grand cost-saving measure. He would take us out in the evening at the golf course at Elk River on hole 16. We would walk along the river and if he saw a ball, he would convince me to go wading in to retrieve it! He learned that golf clubs and ball retrievers could not match the abilities of motivated grandchildren and it gave him an advantage of getting "lost golf balls". If you ever rode in his golf cart you would see dozens and dozens of these noodles, Wilsons, and other golf balls that he delighted in not paying for.

As we got older, we all moved on from collecting golf balls but still wanted to connect with Papa. Chats with Papa were always invigorating, if sometimes one-sided—he had a story for everything, and his knowledge of history was encyclopedic.

It's hard to think we've had our last chats with him. I know this fall I'll be sad to see the Panthers play knowing I won't get to share the highs and lows—mostly lows—of being a Panthers fan with him.

Papa had nearly a century of life on this earth with a fulfilling career, marriage to the love of his life, and treasured friendships that meant the world to him.

This frugal, loving, ambitious, playful, and powerful presence will live on in the memories that my siblings, cousins, and I are so lucky to share. Thank you.

———

Eulogy by Phil Kirk

Mrs. Broyhill, you look as beautiful today as you did the first time I met you more than 60 years ago, Marilyn and Bob, Ed and Melanie, six grandchildren, 13 great grandchildren, other family members and friends.

Over the years when I prepared to introduce Senator James Thomas Broyhill, I asked friends what words they would use to describe him.

You've already heard some of them. Honest, ethical, sincere, intelligent, loyal, hardworking, dedicated, compassionate.

While Senator Broyhill was widely praised for his constituent service, and rightly so, he compiled a remarkable legislative record. Although he never served in the majority in his 23 years in the House of Representatives, he became the Republican leader of the powerful Energy and Commerce committee. When I went to DC to serve as his Chief of Staff for seven years, I was impressed that the Senator told me on several Fridays that he was leaving the office to go on an environmental field trip. That made sense because his committee considered important environmental issues. After hearing that excuse for his Friday absences from the office, I realized his environmental field trip was playing golf!

Speaking of golf, Senator Broyhill allowed me to play golf with him only one time while I was working for him. In fact, Senator Burr, that is where I first met you. Normally it takes between four and five hours to play 18 holes. We finished in 2 1/2 hours and we played through every foursome on the course.

It was in his committee work that he gained a reputation for hard work and the ability to work across the aisle. It was Senator Broyhill who led the fight to pass much of President Ronald Reagan's agenda to deregulate a number of industries, such as telecommunications which allowed the expansion of the cable TV industry.

He was President Reagan's primary partner in the creation of the federal Energy Department, as well as the elimination of many unnecessary and costly regulations.

Senator Broyhill strongly believed in the importance of constituent service. He often met with new members of Congress to counsel them on this priority. Congressman Richard Hudson told me that Senator Broyhill met with him one-on-one to teach him the importance of constituent service.

Thousands of his constituents lived better lives because he and his staff secured Social

Security disability and veterans benefits and passports for them. Staff used to tease him that he worked harder to solve problems for Democrats who would never vote for him than he did for members of his own party. That, of course, was not the case. He treated everyone alike.

He earned the title as Father of the modern-day Republican Party in North Carolina. He was gerrymandered several times in unsuccessful efforts to defeat him. Because he treated all citizens fairly and without regard to race, gender, socio-economic status or political affiliation, Senator Broyhill made it respectable to be a Republican in North Carolina.

Dr. Michael Walden, NC State professor emeritus, recently told me that Senator Broyhill is on the Mt. Rushmore of North Carolina's public servants. I would say that he is at the very top.

If the Senator had instructed me on what to say about him today, there are two stories he would insist that I tell. One was that I opposed him in the Republican primary in 1962 when he first ran for Congress. Actually I had never heard of him, and my county GOP chairman was also in the race, so I supported him out of loyalty. The furniture executive from Lenoir defeated the candidate I supported with at least 80 percent of the vote. I contacted the Broyhill campaign office and assured all who would listen that the Teen Age Republicans in Rowan County would be campaigning for him. We distributed Broyhill sugar scoops and brochures to more than 5,000 households and he upset the incumbent by 1,200 votes. So, I would say that the Senator was a forgiving person.

The second story had to do with a letter I drafted to go with the opinion survey which we sent to every voter in his district. I was pleased that he wrote OK on the draft and did not change a single word, which was unusual. For some reason, the same letter went back to his desk a second time. He read it again and changed EVERY word except, "Dear Friends" and "With warmest regards!"

Time does not permit me to list all his civic, religious, and philanthropic contributions, so permit me to simply say that Senator Broyhill was a leader in many organizations and education and transportation bond issues across our state.

Before I introduce the next speaker, I would like to read a poem which the Senator read at his sister Bettie's funeral and at his sister-in-law Faye Arnold Broyhill's funeral. I hope I can get through the reading of this poem....

GOD ONLY TAKES THE BEST

It's lonesome here without you
We miss you more each day.
Life doesn't seem the same
Since you went away.
When days are sad and lonely
And everything goes wrong
We seem to hear you whisper
"Cheer up and carry on."
Each time we see your picture
You seem to smile and say:
"Don't cry for me. I'm in God's keeping.
We'll meet again someday!"

God saw you were getting tired
And a cure was not to be,
So he put his arms around you
And whispered: "Come with me."
With tearful eyes we watched you suffer,
And saw you fade away.
Although we loved you dearly
We could not make you stay.
A golden heart stopped beating,
Hardworking hands at rest.
God broke our hearts
To prove He only takes the best. AMEN

Senator Broyhill used to end many of his speeches with this comment:

> There are three ingredients for a successful campaign (and I would add
> for many other areas of life).
> Number one is hard work.
> Number two is hard work.
> Number three is hard work.

I can think of no better way to honor the memory of Senator James Thomas Broyhill
than to work hard for the good of our state, nation, and world.

Eulogy by Dr. Michael B. Brown

Winston-Salem, NC, Centenary United Methodist Church, Feb. 28, 2023

Memorial Service for Senator Jim Broyhill

Psalm 121:1-2 … "I will lift up my eyes unto the hills. From whence does my help come? My help comes from the Lord Who made Heaven and earth."
John 14:2-3 … "In My Father's house are many rooms … I go and prepare a place for you. And I will return again and receive you unto Myself, that wheresoever I am, there you may be also."

Across the years since I have known Senator Broyhill, Louise, and their family, he frequently tried to help me out. Often, he sent me emails with jokes, no doubt to lift my spirits. (As is the case with elected officials, so it is with preachers that almost never does someone walk into your office to tell you how happy they are.) Additionally, throughout our years in New York City, Jim would send emails containing religious articles. Those were consistently entitled: "This Will Preach!" I could sense he felt I needed all the help I could get.

Apparently, that never changed. During my last conversation with the Senator, Marilyn, Ed, and I proposed legislation that he should stick around longer. Our society needs people like him. He voted against that proposal. He was ready to begin his next adventure. For some time, he had been composing his memoirs. He said to me from his hospital bed: "Preaching my funeral won't be difficult at all. I've already done all the hard work for you."

So, pretty much everything I'm going to say are things he wrote or were written about him by staff members and friends – most of it from his memoirs.

[1] JIM CARED ABOUT HIS CONSTITUENTS – all of them! Phil Kirk (his Chief of Staff) said that as a Congressman, Jim Broyhill worked as hard for his Democrat constituents as for his Republican ones. That was true. It didn't matter what was your party, age, color, or income. If you were in his district, he believed that your life and well-being were his responsibility, and you knew you could count on him. Where did Jim learn an altruistic principle like that? I think it was from his faith in Jesus Who taught: "You shall love your neighbor as yourself." Jim believed those words and put them to practice.

In his memoirs, Jim talked about his relationships with people he knew and liked [2] ON BOTH SIDES OF THE AISLE. I heard him say once he always tried to listen to his opponents respectfully. "If both of us listen," he said, "I may learn something from them, and they may learn something from me." In his memoirs he wrote that he tried never to think of those who saw things differently as his enemy. "I try to keep the door open," he wrote, "because even if I don't get their vote on this bill, I want to be able to go back to them on the next one." To listen respectfully. "Be ye kind one to another," it says in Ephesians. Wouldn't the world be a better place if we could all learn that bit of wisdom that Jim seemed to know intuitively?

When it came to his personal life (in politics and everywhere else), Jim Broyhill was [3] A MAN OF INTEGRITY AND CHARACTER, A MAN OF HONOR AND PRINCIPLES, a man who when he said something, you never had to wonder whether or not it was true. We need more people like that nowadays. Here's what I think set Jim apart from so many others. Some elected officials see themselves as political leaders. Jim Broyhill saw himself as a public servant. There is a profound difference. Where did he learn that sacred lesson? Again, I think it was from his relationship with Jesus Who said: "The Son of Man has come not to be served, but to serve." Jim Broyhill understood the wisdom of that.

One of the many things I deeply respected about him was his passion for being [4] AN ADVOCATE. Jim knew everybody. Presidents. Kings. Captains of industry and education. People who helped build and strengthen the system of capitalism to which he was unfailingly committed. He would refer to people casually who most of us know only from history books or TV news. But what I found exemplary was that he spoke with equal passion about anonymous folks, like a family living at the end of a dirt road in a holler in Caldwell or Watauga County, people who felt they had run out of hope. "Our farm has been in the family for generations," they would tell him, "but, we don't see any way to save it now." And Jim would work his magic on behalf of people who wouldn't ever be able to pay him back so that their home and land and livelihood were saved. His "payback" was simply the joy he found in helping folks who were not in a position to help themselves. He did that for the poor. For students. For young families. For soldiers. For the elderly.

He also advocated for the workers at Broyhill Furniture. Jim started a Human Resources Department there, training supervisors with the words: "Occasionally you'll have to be firm, but always I expect you to be fair!" His employees were loyal because they were treated fairly.

He advocated for people in the High Country (which those who live there call "God's country" with good reason). "I lift up my eyes unto the hills," was a lesson he wanted read today because in those hills he saw God in a plethora of ways. As one who spends several months annually in those mountains, I told him once: "Jim, you can't drive two miles up here without seeing your family's name … on highways, community centers, buildings at App State or Caldwell Community College, a golf course your family built so those who couldn't afford green fees could still enjoy the game, or parks and nature reserves (Jim was, as you know, a committed environmentalist who took the teachings of the first chapter of Genesis seriously at that point). I told him: "You can't look anywhere in the High Country without seeing your name!" That might have stimulated a bit of vanity in some folks, but not Jim. He just grinned and said: "Well, just as long as you don't see my picture on the wall of the post office!"

Let me mention only two things more (and I promise to be brief). Jim loved his country, his state, and the people who depended on him, but he also had deep and abiding love for [5] HIS FAMILY. I think every time he mentioned Louise to me, he would say: "You know, I married above myself." I didn't know how to answer that except to agree with him. He knew how she held the home together, served as elegant first lady, worked alongside him in campaigns, and provided mooring and security in his personal life. He wrote about that in his memoirs, calling her his "gorgeous bride." Again, his witness at that point reminds me of the word of Jesus: "For this reason a man shall leave his parents and be joined to his wife, and the two shall become one." He also deeply and dearly loved his children and grandchildren. Occasionally he would tell me a story about one of you. At the beginning there would be that dry little grin of his. But by the end of the story his whole face would be beaming with pride. On occasions such as this, not every family is always sure of the love the deceased held for them. But you will never have to doubt his love for a minute. What a sacred gift that is.

Finally, Jim was a man of enduring [6] FAITH. That's how he concluded his memoirs, with a statement of thanks to God for allowing him to make the journey of life. As I said starting out, in our last conversation I asked him to stick around a little longer. But all of us gathered at his bedside could tell his mind was made up. He was ready. And he did not demonstrate one ounce of fear … because he believed the words you heard read earlier: "In My Father's house are many rooms. I go to prepare a place for you. And, I will return again and receive you unto Myself, that wheresoever I am, there you may be also."

In his memoirs, Jim wrote: "Allow love to rule your life." That was, I think, the secret of his noble legacy. He knew that nothing matters more than love, and again he learned that lesson from Jesus Who taught it. The only time Christ ever used the word "command" as an imperative verb was in the Upper Room just before He was crucified. He said: "This I command you, that you love people." Jim built his whole life on that principle. And so when the end came, he knew it was merely the beginning of another journey to be made hand-in-hand with the One in Whom he believed, the One Whose call to Love had fashioned Jim's entire existence.

James Broyhill: North Carolinian, public servant, advocate for the people, defender of democracy, loving husband, father, and grandfather, devoted friend, man of honor, follower of Christ. Tom Campbell, the esteemed journalist from our state, wrote this past week: "We'll probably not see the likes of Jim again … The best and most lasting tribute we could pay him would be to learn from him, to live as he lived and to serve as he served." May it be so.

————

Eulogy by Governor Jim Martin

Wow, what an honor to share this power-filled pulpit this morning.

James Thomas Broyhill, family man, church man, man of the people. A proper epitaph begins with the most important commitments and a devout Christian knows that family and family unity is the key to everything else. I'm thinking of what Laura described: family in 360 degrees. All that he learned from Mr. Ed Broyhill and Miss Sadie growing up alongside his brothers and sisters was the foundation of his long and devoted marriage to our dear Louise. It was faithfully passed down to Marilyn, Philip, and Edgar, and through them to six grandchildren and they've got their work cut out for them. And yes, to Phil Kirk, who served him as faithfully as any man could devote his life to another. And to each of you in turn, what a tribute to have the extended family here today. Which brings us to his chosen vocation.

It is truly written by Phil Kirk that Jim Broyhill was "Father of the Republican Party," which makes Mr. Ed our paternal grandfather. A national committeeman tradition continued in Edgar. Jim not only made it respectable to be a Republican; he made it respectable to be a politician. I know now you're going to say, "Oh wait, wait, whoa." He was a statesman, but you see to get there, it helps to be successful in politics. So, when I arrived in Washington in December 1972, he already had Phil in their office coaching mine, getting us ready. And then this ten-year veteran showed me that he could see through my confident youthful facade, that I could use a bit of humility. He showed me the ropes while Louise comforted Dottie. You see, it's a pretty strange place up there.

Then after he and I survived the 1974 post-Watergate tsunami, I'll tell you I was stunned when he wanted me to seek membership on what I knew only vaguely was referred to as the "powerful Ways and Means Committee." What? What do they do? Taxes. I don't know anything about taxes. He just smiled and said, "You still know how to study, Professor?" It turned out that the Republican committee on committees had decided to make appointments that year in reverse alphabetical order, so my preference, the Appropriations Committee, would come next to last before Agriculture, and his Ways and Means preference would come first. Now guess who represented the entire Southeast on the Republican committee on committees? Right, Jim Broyhill. He told me, "North Carolina needs someone on Ways and Means." Well, I guess I qualified as someone. He said we had not had a tax writer since Bob Doughton [Alleghany County, NC] was chairman of Ways and Means in the '30s and '40s and in 1935 he agreed to sponsor Roosevelt's new Social Security program. The price for that for FDR? Well, you see there was this little Works Progress Administration project to build something called the Blue Ridge Parkway over there in Tennessee. Somehow, turned out it got built over here in the Old North State instead.

For me, it led to a unique opportunity to work on President Reagan's 1981 tax cuts. Of course, its author, Jack Kemp, you see, was not on the Ways and Means committee. He was on Appropriations, so I was among some of the Ways and Means folks who served as what he called his "agents provocateurs." He never told me what that meant. In my last term, Jim helped me get elected to a party leadership position, one of five chairmen of the Republican Research Committee. And it was just in time to head off a legislative unilateral freeze on strategic weapons and this saved President Reagan a stronger hand for negotiating a treaty with the Soviet Union.

You know, Jim was always encouraging. I remember when he invited me for a round of golf at Elk River, I believe it was, where one of the fairways runs alongside a runway for the airport? Is that the one? Well okay, so I pushed my drive over onto the tarmac of that runway and away it went. It bounced, and it bounced, and it bounced, and I was so embarrassed, but he would have none of that. He wanted me to take pride in my work. He said "Wow! That drive must have gone a thousand yards!"

After Jim Broyhill won the GOP Primary, by the way, before his time that [GOP] was called the "Great Opportunities for Postmaster." You know, if Eisenhower got elected and you were a Republican, you got to be the Postmaster. But after he won the Primary for the United States Senate in 1986, John East's death, man, it was my responsibility to appoint his successor for the four months remaining. Of course, my choice could only be the most widely respected, trusted, and admired Congressman in the entire South. The most widely trusted, respected and admired. It was the best choice for Noth Carolina, but maybe not for Jim's campaign. For one thing, the Senate refused to adjourn in time for us to have campaign events, and you know how Broyhill was conscientious. Duty called first. So, we fell short by a mere 1.8 percent. And that's how it came to be that I was the one who finally put Jim Broyhill in jeopardy. This also opened an opportunity for Phil Kirk to join my administration and also to recruit Jim Broyhill for the Economic Development Board, where he soon became chairman. And in January of 1989, he became Secretary of Commerce to oversee its 25 regulatory and promotional commissions and boards. And this put him in the driver's seat for America's most successful industrial recruiting program among all 50 States.

Along with guiding our trade relations with Europe and Asia, it also gave Secretary Broyhill the reigns for his three new programs that he initiated: promotion of tourism and big-time sports events under the travel council; pioneering an aggressive export program for the North Carolina industry offering free training, worldwide advertising, and opening new trade offices in Toronto and Taipei to go along with the old ones in Tokyo and Dusseldorf. His third big innovation for North Carolina was an educational initiative for workforce preparedness and he recruited Food Lion's CEO, Tom Smith, as its first president. Instead of a bunch of new studies, they took four we already had on the shelf and in eight months had it up and rolling. It put special reliance on our community college system to get our young people ready to work. Smart.

Now in a moment, I will yield the balance of my time to Senator Burr, but I have to say this in closing: To be rather than to seem. Surely our state motto found its exemplary icon in this man, Jim Broyhill. He was my teacher and coach, he was my leader, he was my friend. Thank God that North Carolina and the Broyhill family could raise us such a man. Amen.

————

Eulogy by Senator Richard Burr

"Peace, peace. He is not dead, he does not sleep, he is just awakened from life's dream."

Boy, did Jim Broyhill dream big for all he accomplished. I had the good fortune a couple weeks ago to be a ROMEO [Retired Old Men Eating Out] in that short period, Bill and Jack, to have lunch with Jim. And Jack and Bill and I were there to ask the obvious, "Jim, how are you doing?" At which time Jim started his inquisition of all three of us. He wanted to know about my new job and wanted to know how his buds at 94 and 95 if they were still driving. It turned into a great lunch, didn't it, Penn?

So many goals, so many accomplishments, so many lives impacted by James T Broyhill. Jim Broyhill was the real deal. Phil alluded to constituent service. For all of us who have served since Jim Broyhill, he set the bar so high that it's hard for us to meet. Phil may remember the story that Jim believed that Saturday was Constituent Service Day and his constituents shouldn't have to drive to where he had an office, so he got a trailer and he opened the side of the trailer and put the awning down and Jim Broyhill proceeded to have Constituent Service every Saturday. That sounds like a pretty good idea, doesn't it?

He set the bar for so many of us. Jim Broyhill didn't focus on the popular issues. Jim was focused on issues that had a generational impact to them, as you've heard from most who have spoken today. His colleagues in the United States Senate saw Jim as genuine. They saw him as smart as a fox. He was tough on the issues that required him to be tough and he was flexible on the issues that made this country great. Jim Broyhill was my counselor, he was my critic, he was my mentor but more importantly, he was my friend. I remember calling Jim one day. In the 28 years, we've had some tough times lately and I needed to call my counselor and get some advice and before I could get out of my mouth, Governor, what I was struggling with, Jim said, "God I'm envious of you." And I said "Envious? Nobody in their right mind would be envious of what we're going through." He said "I was there 25 years. I never got to do things like impeachments." You see, Jim really understood the rules and the Constitution and to exercise something that was there—to him, Gosh I'm sorry, I missed it. But you know, he didn't miss it. And today Jim's not going to miss anything that goes on from this point forward.

The day I was sworn into the United States House of Representatives, Jim was more excited than I was, and I remembered as he hung around the office and people got to where they were headed out, Jim saw me alone in the office and he walked in and he shut that door and I thought 'Boy he's going to give me the inside story, he's going to teach me, Ed, the secret handshake or whatever it is in Congress'. And the Senator looked at me and he said this, "I've never met anybody that was defeated for something they didn't say." I've never met anybody that was defeated for something they didn't say. That was something that Jim Broyhill firmly believed. That you weren't an expert on everything, that you didn't have to comment on everything, but you weighed in when what you had to say impacted people positively in this country. Jim Broyhill was never a show horse; he was merely a workhorse.

Now I've got the pleasure of reading the eulogy that was provided by Secretary of State, Jim Baker, Secretary of State for George H.W. Bush, Secretary of the Treasury for Ronald Reagan, Chief of Staff to Ronald Reagan and H.W. Bush:

"To Louise, Ed, Marilyn, and all the Broyhill family, ladies and gentlemen,
I'm sorry I cannot be with you today to celebrate the life and legacy of James Thomas Broyhill, a truly beautiful human being, whose service is an enduring reminder of that which has made our nation such a great one. And perhaps more importantly, Jim serves as an example for a new generation less concerned about getting things done for the American people than they are about assigning blame for problems confronting our country. I first came to know Jim when he was a congressman. We worked closely with President Gerald Ford, and I was the President's Under Secretary of Commerce. I soon came to admire both the work ethic of the congressman from North Carolina as well as his ability to forge policy that both sides of the partisan aisle could support. No one on Capitol Hill outworked Jim Broyhill or focused more on getting results than he did.

"Make no mistake, Jim was a rock-rib Republican and a true conservative who helped turn the state from blue to red, but he was much more interested in advancing policy than he was about scoring political points. As a result, he became a critical ally of the next president, Ronald Reagan, who believed like Jim did, that we gauge our elected officials by what they get done. In many ways, the Gipper and Jim are two peas out of the same pod. Of course, no one was more conservative than President Reagan, but he understood the importance of bipartisanship. So did Jim. As Reagan's White House Chief of Staff, I witnessed firsthand Jim's critical role in helping the administration get legislation through a Democrat[ic] Congress controlled by House Speaker Tip O'Neill. When we faced an impasse, Jim rolled up his sleeves and he went to work. Like President Reagan, Jim understood that our national ideal of "E Pluribus Unum,"— out of many, one—is not simply a hollow slogan as too many Americans seem to feel today. The two of them saw it as a guiding principle for their brand of conservatism. Theirs was a message that is sorely needed today during our period of national anger when politicians would rather yell at each other about who's to blame for our problems than talk with one another about how to solve them. Symbolic of our national anger is the partisan animosity between Republicans and Democrats that has brought Washington to a standstill. We can't seem to get anything done because our government isn't working for us. Jim practiced a critical trait required of our democracy. He carefully listened to friends and foes alike. He wouldn't discount an idea simply because it came from a Democrat. When he saw a policy he thought might work, he pursued it, regardless of its origins. I cannot think of a more important trait for America today than one that defined Jim, and I fear for a nation that forgets the importance of working together like he did. We admired Jim Broyhill, and we will miss him, but we will see him on the other side."

The Secretary knows, as most here who knew Jim Broyhill [know], we expect Jim to greet us at the Gates of Heaven when we arrive. Amen.

———

Eulogy by Randell Jones

I met Senator Broyhill only 20 years ago when I was asked to interview him for a history about the founding of the Overmountain Victory National Historic Trail, the trail being an accomplishment which greatly pleased the Senator, an important part of his legacy of public service. During the following years, the Senator and I were involved in other subsequent projects for this Trail—his Trail, if I may—and I observed then how much the Senator loves America, loves North Carolina, loves his family. And the Senator was kind to write the forewords for my two books about the Battle of Kings Mountain and the Overmountain Victory National Historic Trail.

In those forewords, the Senator wrote of his lifelong affection for the story of the Battle of Kings Mountain—that ferocious confrontation on October 7, 1780, that turned the tide of the American Revolution. He wrote of growing up in a home where he heard stories about that patriot victory, of knowing in the community descendants of the heroes of that battle, and noting that Fort Defiance, the home of one of those heroes, William Lenoir, was in his home county, Caldwell.

But his personal interest in the story of that battle and the Trail went deeper still, the Senator said, because as he wrote, "In 1975, a remarkable group of dedicated citizens came to me as a Member of Congress and asked me to help secure federal recognition of the route these patriots followed out of the mountains to confront the invading British forces." After three years, the bill he sponsored was signed into law by President Jimmy Carter in the fall of 1980, just weeks before the 200th anniversary of that battle. This new legislation made the Overmountain Victory Trail the first national historic trail east of the Mississippi River.

In 2014, the citizen support group, the Overmountain Victory Trail Association, conducted the 40th consecutive, annual reenactment march of the historic trail, as they have continued to do since 1975. During that two-week reenactment march, my friend here, this militiaman statuette, and his twin went along. They travelled the entire length of the 330-mile trail in Virginia, Tennessee, North Carolina, and South Carolina, day by historic day, having their pictures made at each historic site and memorial. That twin brother-in-arms statuette stands proudly today in the Kings Mountain Room at the History Museum of Burke County in Morganton, a gift to the museum in 2020 as a tribute to Senator Broyhill on the 40th anniversary of the Trail's designation by Congress.

That statuette is there because Morganton is the heart of the trail, the home to Quaker Meadows, where a thousand men on horseback and on foot gathered after crossing the snow-covered Appalachian Mountains in a four-day march from the overmountain regions of North Carolina and Virginia. They were joined by 350 militiamen coming up the Yadkin River valley. The leaders gathered under the Council Oak and made plans to pursue the arrogant British Major Patrick Ferguson who had threatened: "If you do not desist your opposition to the British arms, I shall march this army over the mountains, hang your leaders, and lay waste your country with fire and sword."

These men, serving in the organized state militia of North Carolina and Virginia, were joined by men serving in the state militias of South Carolina and Georgia. Together they relentlessly pursued Major Ferguson until 3 o'clock on the afternoon of Saturday, October 7, when they bravely charged up the sides of Little Kings Mountain three times in the face of cold steel, having pledged to each other as Americans: "We will not fail."

They defeated the loyalists troops atop Kings Mountain that day, securing a victory which Thomas Jefferson later called "that joyful annunciation of the turn of the tide of success which terminated the Revolutionary War with the seal of our independence."

I have heard Senator Broyhill tell that story many times over the years to different groups. And in every talk, he was certain to declare in his conclusion: …

… If there had been no Battle of Kings Mountain, there would have been no Battle of Cowpens. If there had been no Cowpens, there would have been no Battle of Guilford Courthouse. And if there had been no Guilford Courthouse, there would have been no Yorktown.

Imagine that—no surrender by the British at Yorktown, no history of American independence, no US Constitution, no Bill of Rights, none of the American liberties we enjoy today. None of that had there been no Battle of Kings Mountain. That is what Senator Broyhill wanted—and wants—every American to know.

And what those of us who also love this story and love this trail believe, and what we want everyone to appreciate, is that there would be no Overmountain Victory National Historic Trail if there had been no James T. Broyhill.

We thank you, sir. And we salute you.

Condolences and Remembrances Shared

Dear Marilyn,

Your father gave me my first job on Capitol Hill as a caseworker, which I loved because it involved solving people's problems. Constituent service was a bedrock of his office, and I loved being part of that. He promoted me beyond where many women were going at that time. He was a part of my life throughout my career and retirement.

I have many fond memories of my time in his office. Here is one of my favorites:

Sometime in the early 1970s, the Smithsonian Folk Festival on the National Mall, held every summer, had a feature on Appalachia. A group of people from (I believe) Watauga County was there demonstrating such things as making soap in a big iron pot, cooking on a wood stove, and even making moonshine. He and I went down to say hello to them on the first day. They were dressed in country clothes, blue jean overalls, long cotton skirts, aprons, etc. He was dressed in a dark suit, white shirt and tie. One lady making corn bread in a wood stove pulled me aside and said, "We just love Jim. He's one of us." And he was. He could identify with everyone.—Excerpt from a letter from Cecile Srodes to Marilyn Broyhill Beach February 28, 2023

My grandfather, Jim Broyhill, passed away yesterday at 95 after a long and full life. I was blessed to have him for so long - I know not many people can say they have grandparents living at my age! Many people will remember him for his public service career but to our family he was just "Papa." He was always proud of having fed me my first solid meal as a baby. As Bobby told him when we said our goodbyes on Friday, "Papa, I hope you've had an awesome time on earth, and I hope you are excited to meet God and Jesus! They are really cool guys!"

—Laura Beach Dugan, Granddaughter

"My Favorite Boss"

Dear Louise, Marilyn, and Ed,

You and your family have been on my mind so much these past weeks as I have mourned the loss of your husband and father.

In 1967, I left my career as an elementary school teacher in the Midwest to begin an adventure and a relocation. I accompanied my friend Barbara to Washington D.C. where she was about to begin her new position at the Library of Congress.

I also needed a job, and my search began with an employment agency. Because I could type and take shorthand, I was sent to Capitol Hill for an interview. I had little interest in politics and had never been to North Carolina, so imagine my shock but also my happiness at having the opportunity to become the "personal secretary" to Congressman James T. Broyhill.

As it turned out, I felt like the luckiest woman in the world to have a job that I grew to love, and to work for a man that I so highly respected and who was genuine and kind. His staff became my extended family. Moreover, who would have guessed that my adventure with Barb, which started all of this, would result in her marrying one of our staff members, Mickey Holton, a couple of years later.

As far as I was concerned, my new office duties suited me perfectly. I am so very grateful for my "best job ever" experience.

Over the years, I have told this story repeatedly, emphasizing how fortunate I was to have met JTB and his very special family.

I learned so much from your husband and father. He was a remarkable human being, and it was a treat of a lifetime to have been able to work for him.

With gratitude, I send lots of hugs and love to you. Richard and I grieve the passing of my favorite boss.—Lynn Clayton Peterson

Dear Marilyn and Ed,

As you both know, your dad meant a great deal to me. Not only was he a joy to work for, he had a profound effect on making me and all of the staff effective and honest, and he brought forth hidden talents in all of us. Yes, we tried to make him look good in the eyes of his constituents. But what an easy task it was because of the man he was. From 1970 through 1986, his office was my home away from home. It was truly special to receive that call from him that Wednesday afternoon. I shed many a tear after that precious call, but I was so happy that I had the chance to tell him personally how much he really meant to me in every way. He and your mother called me personally in 1971 the morning after my mother died. They called me again the morning after my husband died in 2021. Where do you find a man of his stature making calls like that? I got the chance to tell him that he put a light in an otherwise very sad time for me and I won't ever forget it.

In the years that followed, he never hesitated to make reference calls for me even when I didn't ask. I know that put my foot in the door. I also would ask him questions and seek his advice many times.

I can imagine how you both feel. But please know your dad was loved and admired by everyone who got to know him. He is someone I will never forget, and I am so glad that Vince Monzel hired me in 1970 and gave me the opportunity of my life.

I am so sorry, and you have my heartfelt sympathy. I was privileged to also know you and your dear mother.

Much love and hugs to all of you.
Mary Trimble

I was pleased to see this letter in the Saturday "Free for All" page which includes opinion letters from Post readers. I knew the author, Peter Kinzler, and ran into him a couple of years ago at a Nats baseball game. We reminisced about the "good old days", when we were on the Hill and often disagreed but worked together to actually get things done. Reading this very nice letter meant a lot to me.—Cecile Srodes

Washington Post, Letters to the Editor, March 10, 2023
Washington, D.C.

Goodbye to a conservative who reliably crossed the aisle

The Feb. 21 obituary for former congressman Jim Broyhill, "GOP congressman from North Carolina briefly served in the Senate," described him as a "reliable conservative." That did not do justice to his impact on consumer and environmental legislation.

During his long tenure on the House commerce committee, Broyhill was a frequent negotiating partner with committee Democrats. While never compromising his conservative principles, he was able to find the intersection of liberal and conservative ideas to help craft landmark legislation. In addition to his role in the creation of the U.S. Consumer Product Safety Commission, discussed in the obituary, Broyhill also worked with Rep. John Moss (D-Calif.) to pass legislation to revitalize the Federal Trade Commission and with Rep. Bob Eckhardt (D-Tex.) to pass the Toxic Substances Control Act of 1976 that regulates chemicals that pose "an unreasonable risk to health or the environment."

Broyhill's belief that members of goodwill on both sides of the aisle could work together to find ways to improve the lives of their constituents made him one of the most important Republicans who helped make the legislative process work for the public good in the 1970s. More members of both parties in Congress today should approach their jobs in the same way. Peter Kinzler, Alexandria

Published Comments

Obituary for James T. Broyhill

Senator James Thomas Broyhill was born August 19, 1927, in Lenoir, NC and passed away February 18, 2023. He served in the United States Congress for 24 years, both in the House of Representatives and Senate. He began his career in his family's company, Broyhill Furniture Industries, which his father founded.

He entered public service early. He became President of the Lenoir Chamber of Commerce in 1956 and 1957, chaired the Caldwell County Blood Drive in 1957, and was named "Young Man of the Year for Lenoir and Caldwell County" in 1957 by the Lenoir Jaycees. He was Vice-Chairman of the Furniture and Plywood Council of the NC Forestry Association from 1955 to 1962 and was a member of the Lenoir Aviation Club. He was an active member of the First Baptist Church of Lenoir where he taught Sunday School and was a member of the choir.

In 1962, Jim was elected to the US House of Representatives, the first Republican to be elected in his district in the Twentieth Century. During his 23 years' tenure in the House, he represented one third of the state's counties. He was respected by members of both parties both in his district and among his colleagues. Because of this he was effective in legislative accomplishments and advocating for his constituents.

In the House of Representatives, he served on the powerful Interstate and Foreign Commerce Committee (subsequently the Energy and Commerce Committee) where he was ranking minority member, the House Post Office and Civil Service Committee, and the House Small Business Committee. He was awarded "Watchdog of the Treasury" trophies by the National Association for Small Business each year he was in Congress. He sponsored and helped draft many of the major pieces of legislation of the second half of the twentieth century. In 1986 he was appointed by Governor Jim Martin to the US Senate where he served on the Armed Services Committee and the Judiciary Committee.

After leaving Washington he served as Chairman of the North Carolina Board of Economic Development, the Secretary of the North Carolina Department of Commerce, Member and Chair of the Economic Development Committee of NC Citizens for Business and Industry, Co Chairman of the State Bond Drive benefiting NC Schools, Co-Chairman of the State Bond Drive benefiting the NC University System and Community College System and Co-Chairman of the North Carolina Welfare to Work Business Council.

He received the I. E. Ready Award by the NC Community College System for Outstanding work for the Community College system. He was inducted into the North Carolina Republican Party Hall of Fame and the North Carolina Business Hall of Fame. The Lenoir, North Carolina Post Office and a section of US 321 between Hickory and Blowing Rock, NC are named in his honor.

Jim served as Chair of the Board of Trustees at Appalachian State University and Member of the Appalachian State University Foundation Board. He was a member of the boards of directors of the Second Harvest Food Bank of Northwest NC, Senior Services, Inc. in Winston-Salem, and the North Carolina Museum of History Foundation. He was a member of the boards of visitors of the Babcock School of Management, Wake Forest University, and Wake Forest University Baptist Medical Center.

He received an Honorary Doctor of Law from Catawba College, Honorary Degree of Associate in Arts from Richmond Community College, the Order of the Long Leaf Pine Award, and the North Carolina Award in the field of public service, the highest civilian award given by the state.

Jim had an avid interest in history and gave numerous entertaining speeches to civic groups across the state, including one on the Battle of King's Mountain. He was particularly proud of his part in establishing and preserving the over 330-mile-long Overmountain Victory Trail as part of the U S Historic Trails System, in memory of the patriots who marched along the trail to defeat the British in the decisive Battle of King's Mountain on October 7, 1780. Other lectures featured the history of the United States Capitol, and United States Presidents. When visiting Washington in the years following his time in Congress, he delighted in taking friends and family on personalized tours of the Capitol. He was friends with and worked closely with many U.S. Presidents over the years. His congressional career spanned the presidencies of John F. Kennedy to Ronald Reagan.

Throughout his life he loved to recall his idyllic childhood in Lenoir. His community rallied around him when he was nine years old, and he fell into a coma due to a case of rheumatic fever. While he was recovering at home for a year, he developed a lifelong love of reading and music. In High School he was senior class president, drum major in the Lenoir High School Band led by Captain James Harper and played First Flute. He performed with the North Carolina Symphony while only in high school and upon graduation was invited to become a member of the Symphony. Memorable childhood events included a trip to the New York World's Fair in 1939, going with his father to furniture markets in Chicago, and a transatlantic voyage to Europe on the Ocean Liner Queen Elizabeth, just after the end of World War II.

His favorite recreation was golf. He had an outstanding singing voice, and was a voracious reader, especially of American History. His sharp mind was able to recall minute details, and he could recite all U.S. Presidents and Vice Presidents forward and backward. Even in his 90s, he could name the reigning English monarch for any given year in the last thousand years. He rarely missed an episode of Jeopardy. For many years he entertained his friends in the Romeo Club (Retired Old Men Eating Out) with well-timed jokes and anecdotes.

He is survived by his wife of 71 years, Louise Horton Robbins of Durham, NC. They met in 1949 at a party at his fraternity, Phi Delta Theta, at the University of North Carolina at Chapel Hill. A few weeks later he saw her waiting at a bus stop and offered her a ride. After his graduation in 1950, he stopped frequently to visit Louise at Chapel Hill and her home in Durham while calling on furniture customers in eastern North Carolina. They were married shortly after her graduation in 1951, and made their home in Lenoir, where within 5 years their three children were born. Jim and Louise were true partners throughout their seven decades of marriage, in both their lives in public service and at home. He always remarked on how lucky he was that a beautiful girl like her agreed to go out with him that fateful day in 1949, and every day, wherever they were, he said she was the prettiest in the room.

Independent Tribune, Feb. 22, 2023
by Tom Campbell

In the Pantheon of notable North Carolina public servants, none stands so tall as Jim Broyhill.

The Broyhill family story is essentially the North Carolina story. Starting from humble beginnings, family members learned to work hard, persevere, be humble and serve others.

Jim's father started at age 11, working as a blacksmith, lumberman, logger and ultimately furniture maker. Ed Broyhill's mantra was, "God forges us on an anvil of adversity for a purpose known only to him." He started Lenoir Chair Company to provide low-priced furniture. It evolved into Broyhill Industries with a payroll of 7,500.

Ed Broyhill was a Republican in the era when our state was overwhelmingly Democratic. Just about every big-name national Republican came to Lenoir to discuss politics with Ed. Jim Broyhill remembers many discussions around the family kitchen table. Not only did he listen, but they helped to form his own political philosophy.

After graduating from Carolina, Jim came into what was by then a successful family enterprise, learning the business and making his mark by helping develop a highly successful national sales force. He also adopted the family value in giving back and serving others, becoming a leader in his local chamber, community endeavors and national furniture trade associations.

He fell in love and married the beautiful and gracious Louise and started a family, but politics was always a strong interest and in 1962 he made his first foray into becoming a candidate.

The Democratic controlled legislature wanted to rid the state of the only Republican in our Congressional delegation, Charles R. Jonas. After the 1960 census, Democratic legislators figured a way to eliminate Jonas by gerrymandering his congressional district, moving many of his Republican voters into a new district. This backfired on them because in so doing, they formed a new ninth district that was more competitive. Jim saw an opportunity and seized it, defeating a five term Democrat. The end result was two Republicans representing our state in Congress.

In Washington, the young Carolinian quietly and deliberately learned how things worked in congress and how to get things accomplished by making allies in both parties. He landed a spot on the House Commerce Committee and it became the launching pad to create a record of effectiveness rarely seen by a North Carolina representative

Epilogue

from either party. Congressman Broyhill was effective in enlisting members of both parties to sponsor and pass significant legislation.

People in the foothills or our state will tell you Broyhill's most important contribution was that he "wrote the book" on outstanding constituent service. I remember well that whenever those of us in broadcasting had a position or needed to get legislation passed, Jim Broyhill was the first call made. He was always willing to listen, consider, and if he thought an idea worthy, would pursue it. We weren't alone. It's no wonder he was re-elected 10 times by huge margins, converting his congressional district into the highest Republican registration in the state.

In July 1986, Gov. Jim Martin prevailed on Broyhill to fill an unexpired U.S. Senate term and he complied. After losing the seat in the November election (the only election he ever lost), Jim returned to Lenoir, but not for long. Martin asked him to serve as Secretary of Commerce and he was influential in attracting new business to our state. Upon his retirement, he remained active, especially in the Broyhill Foundation's efforts to help others.

But merely citing Jim Broyhill's record, outstanding as it was, doesn't help us understand the man. He remained a stalwart Republican, but not today's loud, headline-seeking, combative and divisive kind. He always looked to involve himself in the betterment of our state and in making a positive difference. No wonder leaders from both parties who knew Jim Broyhill are paying glowing tributes to him in death.

To be welcomed into Jim and Louise's home was to see grace and hospitality in action. Yes, there were a plethora of pictures displaying the Broyhills with presidents and politicians, but just as many of his family and times together. I was privileged to spend time with him in 2012, producing a 90-minute television interview with him and having him recall his life and times. It was a rich moment with this hero of mine. He was so humble he would deflect accolades and or recognition of his achievements. That was Jim Broyhill.

Jim Broyhill was a citizen of the nation, a cheerleader for our state and a mentor for many.
We will not likely see Jim's likes again. Webster would be hard pressed to amass enough superlatives to describe this son of North Carolina. The best and most lasting tribute we could pay him would be to learn from him, to live as he lived and serve as he served.

The Salisbury Post, February 28, 2023
by Phil Kirk

Then-Congressman Jim Broyhill and later Senator Jim Broyhill visited Rowan County many times in the 60's when he represented our county in the U. S. Congress. He brought many important people to Rowan County, including Richard Nixon, Gerald Ford, Bob Dole, Strom Thurmond, and many others.

My political career and 60-year friendship with Jim and Louise Broyhill began in an unusual way. He was involved in a Republican primary in 1962 with Les Burdick, Rowan GOP chairman, for the nomination to face incumbent Congressman Hugh Alexander. I was President of the East Rowan Teen Age Republicans and was working closely with party chairman Burdick, so I was loyal to him and supported him in the primary. I had never met Senator Broyhill at the time.

Senator Broyhill beat Burdick in a landslide receiving more than 80 percent of the vote. The older Republicans in Rowan County were bitter about the outcome, and many declined to support the Broyhill candidacy. I called the Broyhill campaign office a few days after the primary and promised that the Teen Age Republicans would campaign door-to-door for him in Rowan County. We knocked on more than 5,000 doors and left campaign brochures and Broyhill sugar scoops! He won the election by 1200 votes.

Mary Cridlebaugh, my history teacher at East Rowan who now lives in Thomasville, reminded me recently that the newly elected Jim Broyhill visited our history class the day after his upset victory in November 1962. She wrote, "I no longer remember what he said, but I do remember being impressed that he had come from Lenoir and probably had no sleep since learning the results of the election. He had to have been pretty tired." That is a good example of Senator Broyhill's work ethic and also keeping his promise that if he won, he would be at East Rowan High the next day.

Democrats in the North Carolina General Assembly tried to defeat our state's only Republican Congressman Charles R. Jonas in 1962 by putting several of his Republican-leaning counties in Alexander's district and adding Democratic strongholds to Jonas's district. Our state ended up with two Republicans, Jonas and Broyhill, in Congress. After having Senator Broyhill as our Congressman for three terms, the Democrats tried again with their partisan gerrymandering in an effort to defeat him. What happened? The voters rebelled again and elected two more Republican Congressmen, Dr. Earl Ruth of Salisbury and Wilmer "Vinegar Bend" Mizell of Davidson County!

The Broyhills spent a lot of time in Rowan County, campaigning at the county fair, riding in the Faith Fourth of July parade, visiting every nook and cranny in search of votes, and they made many life-long friends here. Catawba College gave Senator Broyhill an Honorary Doctor of Laws degree and he was very proud of that. He carried Rowan County by a 3-1 margin before the Democrats removed Rowan County from his district. Bob Andrew of Faith was on the Broyhill team from the very beginning and served as his chairman in Rowan County. He was nicknamed the "Candy Man" because he owned a wholesale candy company!

Senator Broyhill, who was in the House at the time, convinced me to come to Capitol Hill to serve as his Chief of Staff and I did so from 1977-84 between serving similar roles with former Governors Jim Holshouser and Jim Martin. That was a great experience and resulted in an even closer friendship with the Broyhill family.

Senator Broyhill strongly believed in the importance of constituent service. He and his staff worked hard to get Social Security disability and veteran's benefits for those who deserved them. He often met one-on-one with new Republican members of Congress to emphasize the importance of quality constituent service. Congressman Richard Hudson, who represented Rowan County at one point, told me that Broyhill emphasized this important aspect of being a congressman in an early session with him.

While he never served in the majority in the House, his work ethic and ability to work with both Democrats and Republicans made him a successful member of Congress. He worked with presidents of both parties. As the Republican leader (called the ranking member) of the Energy and Commerce committee, he worked closely with President Ronald Reagan to de-regulate a number of industries, including telecommunications de-regulation which allowed cable TV to flourish. The Reagan/Broyhill team was instrumental in the formation of the Department of Energy. Senator Broyhill worked tirelessly to get rid of unnecessary, costly regulations throughout the federal government.

Often when I introduced Broyhill to many groups over the years, I asked people what words came to mind when they heard the name "Senator Broyhill?" Responses included honest, ethical, sincere, intelligent, loyal, hardworking, dedicated, compassionate. I knew that I would never be embarrassed nor disappointed to say that I was a friend of Jim Broyhill.

Senator Broyhill used to end many of his speeches with this comment. "There are three ingredients for a successful campaign (and I would add for many other areas of life). Number one is hard work. Number two is hard work. And number three is hard work."

I can think of no better way for us to honor the memory of Senator James Thomas Broyhill than to work hard for the good of our state, nation, and world.

AP NEWS
N. Carolina congressman, briefly senator Broyhill dies at 95
by Gary D. Robertson
February 18, 2023

RALEIGH, N.C. (AP) — Jim Broyhill, a longtime North Carolina Republican congressman who served briefly in the U.S. Senate to fill a vacancy before losing a bid to keep the job, died early Saturday at age 95, his family said.

Broyhill, a scion of the Broyhill Furniture business in the North Carolina foothills that brought jobs and prestige to the region, died at Arbor Acres retirement home in Winston-Salem, according to his son, Ed. He had suffered from congestive heart failure for years that worsened in recent months, his son said Saturday.

The moderate Republican served more than 23 years in the House. He was considered a reliable conservative who helped North Carolina turn into a competitive two-party state, particularly as the GOP made national gains in the 1980s with Ronald Reagan.

In a video interview in honor of receiving a state award in 2015, Broyhill recalled the dearth of Republicans on the first state ballot he filled out in 1948.

"I was determined that I'm going to do what I could to see if we could not develop a two-party system in our state," Broyhill said. "And I think I had a great deal to accomplish that, but with the help and the leadership of many other people."

GOP Gov. Jim Martin appointed Broyhill to replace Republican Sen. John East when East died by suicide in June 1986.

Broyhill had already won the Senate GOP primary a month earlier against David Funderburk, who had the support of Sen. Jesse Helms' national organization that backed hardline Republicans. East wasn't seeking reelection due to medical issues.

The Senate appointment was viewed as an asset to help Broyhill in his fall general election against former Gov. Terry Sanford, a Democrat and outgoing Duke University president. Sanford narrowly defeated Broyhill in two elections that November -- one to serve out the rest of 1986 and another for the next six years.

Expected initially to be a low-key affair, the campaign took on the intensity of a modern, more divisive campaign. Reagan came to Charlotte to campaign for Broyhill. In a recent interview, Martin said he's unsure whether appointing Broyhill to the Senate ultimately aided his campaign.

"He wasn't able to spend as much time campaigning because he was intensely dependable on fulfilling his Senate duties," Martin said.

Broyhill's Capitol Hill career began with a surprising U.S. House victory in 1962. When Democrats attempted to redraw the district of the lone Republican in the House delegation after the 1960 census in hopes of defeating him, the adjoining district became more Republican, according to a biography of Martin. That opened the door for Broyhill, who had worked at the family business for close to two decades, to upset Democratic incumbent Hugh Quincy Alexander.

While he never served in a Republican-controlled chamber until his Senate appointment, Broyhill flexed his political muscles for Republican presidential administrations in the House and built support for their agendas with Democrats.

In the interview highlighting his 2015 award, Broyhill recalled legislation he helped pass to create the U.S. Consumer Product Safety Commission. Broyhill's family and others cited his efforts to create energy policies, and deregulate the telecommunications, pharmaceutical and trucking industries.

Frank Drendel, founder of coaxial cable producer CommScope based in Hickory, said on Saturday that Broyhill's work to get a law passed in 1978 so that cable companies could connect their cables to other utility poles helped the cable industry soar. Broyhill "set an example that sadly we don't have much of today and that is to cross the aisle and come up with solutions that are nonpartisan," said former Glaxo Wellcome CEO Bob Ingram, a North Carolina resident who knew Broyhill while working in Washington. "He wanted to get to the best answer to solve problems."

After his 1986 defeat, Broyhill served on North Carolina's Economic Development Board. Martin later picked him to serve in his second-term Cabinet as commerce secretary, saying he had "impeccable connections with North Carolina industry."

A native of Lenoir, James Thomas Broyhill graduated from the University of North Carolina at Chapel Hill in 1950, according to his official congressional biography. His father, J.E. Broyhill, began the family's furniture dynasty in 1926 as the Lenoir Chair Company and was a well-known Republican in his own right.

"Jim added to that and made his contribution in a huge way as a member of Congress," Martin said. "That family tradition has given an enormous boost to the Republican Party." Ed Broyhill is now a Republican National Committee member.

Recently retired Sen. Richard Burr, R-N.C., who was recruited by Broyhill to run for Congress more than 30 years ago, said he would be remembered as "a gentlemen and a statesman," and called him a "mentor and confidant."

"I always knew I could trust his advice and counsel because he viewed everything through the lens of what's best for the country," Burr said.

Current Democratic Gov. Roy Cooper praised Broyhill on Saturday in a tweet for his commitment and service to the state.

The congressman was preceded in death by his son, Philip. In addition to Ed Broyhill, other survivors of Broyhill include his wife of 71 years, Louise R. Broyhill; his daughter, Marilyn Broyhill Beach of Winston-Salem; six grandchildren and 13 great-grandchildren.

Broyhill's funeral will be Feb. 28 at Centenary United Methodist Church in Winston-Salem, with a graveside service later that day in Wilkes County.

Honor guard from the Overmountain Victory Trail Association
at the graveside ceremony in Boomer, North Carolina

U.S. Senator James Thomas Broyhill
August 19, 1927 - February 18, 2023

Printed in the USA
CPSIA information can be obtained
at www.ICGtesting.com
LVHW061318110724
784709LV00002B/8